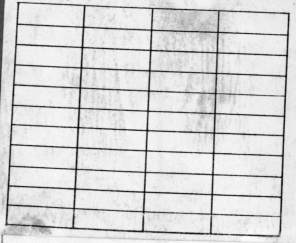

# THE NEW GOLF FOR WOMEN

# THE NEW GOLF FOR WOMEN

### Edited by John Coyne

A Rutledge Book

Doubleday & Company, Inc.
New York

Our thanks to Bud Erickson, executive director of the Ladies Professional Golf Association, for his cooperation in preparing this book.

Photography by Melchior DiGiacomo

ISBN: 0-385-00849-X
Library of Congress Catalog Card Number: 72-82975
© 1973 by Rutledge Books, Inc.
Prepared and produced by Rutledge Books, Inc.
Printed in the United States of America
Doubleday & Company, Inc.
277 Park Avenue
New York, New York 10017

# Foreword

I am very happy to have been asked to write a foreword for *The New Golf for Women*.

As a player and now a teacher, I can quite honestly say that whereas playing is a skill, teaching is an art. A player may be a great striker of the ball, yet be unable to communicate his knowledge to another person to help him improve his game. The transition from player to teacher is a difficult one. Teaching requires the knack of putting yourself in the pupil's position and then finding a way to solve that pupil's golfing problem. A teacher is the direct opposite of a player, who is constantly thinking about himself and his particular problems.

As has often been said before, what women golfers lack in strength, they must make up for in the precise execution of golfing fundamentals. I have noticed that today's women golfers are constantly seeking ways of improving their play. As a result, many of them will, in time, attain enough skill to become the professional teachers so sorely needed by this great game.

The professionals selected for *The New Golf for Women* have the knowledge and experience to put together a book that will help all golfers, and that is what they have done. All are excellent players. I have watched, taught and played with many of them. I know that they are "in touch" with the game and with its new, improved methods of playing and teaching. They are totally dedicated not only to competing well but also to teaching well.

Women's golf has risen to great heights in recent years. There is today an unprecedented enthusiasm on the part of women for learning and playing the game. And the future looks bright for woman teachers of golf. The time is right.

The professionals in this book have mastered golf. They understand the game, both emotionally and scientifically. They approach the game from sound physical, geometric, dynamic and psychological perspectives. Listen to them. They can improve anyone's golfing.

Bob Toski

# Contents

Introduction    11

Chapter 1
From Tee to Green
by Kathy Whitworth    17

Chapter 2
Driving for Distance
by Betty Burfeindt    55

Chapter 3
Playing the Woods
from Fairway and Rough
by Judy Rankin    71

Chapter 4
Playing the Long Irons to Score
by Sandy Haynie    95

Chapter 5
Playing the Short Irons
by Sandy Palmer    109

Chapter 6
Playing the Wedge
from Grass and Sand
by Mary Mills    131

Chapter 7
Putting on and off the Green
by Pam Barnett    171

Chapter 8
Playing the Trouble
Shots with Control
by Jane Blalock    195

Chapter 9
Golf Clinic    215

# Introduction

This is a new book for women to read and to identify with. It is a book of golf instruction written solely for women by members of the Ladies Professional Golf Association. Usually we must read golf instruction books by men, and their advice does not always apply to us. There are, of course, some articles in golf publications written and illustrated by women, but they are very, very few.

Many women across the country have asked where they might take lessons from a lady professional and whether there are lady professionals who teach. These women tell me that since they feel a man wouldn't understand their problems as well as a woman, they would not feel as comfortable asking him questions as they would her.

This book gives these women—and other women just starting out in golf—a chance to see someone of their sex accomplishing what they are trying to do. Golf is a woman's game. It does not require a tremendous amount of strength. It is not a contact sport. It is a sport in which women, by using a longer club, can drive the ball just as far as the men.

It is a sport in which a woman has natural advantages. One of these advantages is sensitivity—a kind of perception that gets down into her fingertips and comes out when she's holding a putter. She "feels" her game more strongly than a man.

For instance, when someone asks me how hard I stroke a 16-foot putt, I've got to answer, "I don't know. I look at the ball; I look at the cup; I take in the kind of roll I've got. And when I've done this, I just *feel* I've got to hit the ball a certain way." This "feeling" is the most important factor in a woman's game.

For women beginning golf, I stress the fundamentals. It's a mistake simply to pick up a club and start swinging. Take lessons from a competent professional—it's worth the money! Don't be in a hurry to get onto the golf course. The more time you spend on the practice tee or at a driving range, the better your actual style of play will be. Get your swing down before going out on the course.

Almost any woman can play golf. It doesn't matter how young or old you are. Nor does it matter what size you are. To some extent, size will be a factor in the length of your shots, but here again, work on coordination can do much to make up for a lack of power. And some of our smallest women on the tour are the long hitters—Judy Rankin and Sandy Palmer, for examples.

Women also have certain psychological advantages in the game of golf. A man is expected to pick up a club and break 90 before he's spent 20 hours on the course. A woman is not expected to be so adept, since she is usually considered helpless, unable to hit the ball.

Fortunately, that's no longer true. Not in the age of women's liberation. Women have proved they can do just about anything men can. They certainly can play golf as well as men, but they are doing it in their own way.

For example, women who play golf must develop a stronger hip movement. This is where our power is—in the hips and legs. Men have stronger arms, more powerful shoulders. They can make a golf shot work using just these two parts of their body. Women, however, need the additional strength of hips and legs.

Women must also understand the game well enough to select the right clubs for themselves, not only in length and weight but also in number. Most of the professional women are now using the five-wood. This club gives them extra power and makes up for a lack of strength.

Golf is really three games. There's the long game, in which women can be at a disadvantage. There's the short game, in which women are at no disadvantage at all; in fact, if they've worked on their coordination and perception, they are ahead of that game by a mile. And then there is the game that is really 18 games in one. Each hole is a miniature golf game, an individual challenge, an individual chance to "feel" the pitfalls of the course and attempt to beat the odds. Women are marvelous at this kind of thinking. A woman can and does think of a particular hole (say a par 5) as a small world in itself. Women respond to these individual challenges very well, and by scoring well on one hole after the other, they can score well for 18 holes.

In the following chapters, the finest pros in the game discuss an area of golf in which each is outstanding. These women are the new, young professionals on the tour. They have all been well trained in the game, and they have been playing golf almost since they began to walk. In my section I discuss the golf game from tee to green, concentrating on the fundamentals. Then seven of my fellow touring professionals discuss in detail individual aspects of the golf game. It is all here, everything you need to know to play golf or to play golf better.

Kathy Whitworth

# THE NEW
# GOLF FOR
# WOMEN

# Kathy Whitworth
# From Tee to Green

Kathy Whitworth of Richardson, Texas, is the leading money-winner of the LPGA Tour, having won over $396,000. She has won every major women's tournament except the USGA Women's Open. Since turning professional in 1959, Kathy has won 64 tournaments; in 1972 alone, she won 5. Considered one the the great golfers of all time, she has dominated women's golf for 10 years.

Born in 1939, Kathy started golfing at the age of 15. Twice she has been named Woman of the Year by the Associated Press; six times she has earned the Vare Trophy for the lowest scoring average on the tour; and seven times she has been the women's leading money-winner.

In women's golf, Kathy is Arnold Palmer and Jack Nicklaus rolled into one.

**Grip:** Use the overlapping grip on all shots. The little finger of the right hand overlaps the index finger of the left. Keep fingers close together on the shaft of the club. Both Vs formed by thumb and forefinger extension should point between the chin and right shoulder.

**Stance:** Width apart of feet is approximately the same as shoulder width. Weight is distributed equally between both feet, from the ball of the foot to the heel. Feet, hips and shoulders are all square to the line of flight. Knees are bent slightly. The back is kept straight, but tilted slightly forward from the hips. Arms hang naturally to grip the club.

**Swing:** Weight is kept on the inside of both feet with the clubhead moving back low and following the natural turn of the body. The hands, arms, hips, club and weight shift together. Left side starts the movement back to the ball. This is a turning as well as a lateral movement of the left side.

**Club Selection:** Never attempt to press a club (swing hard for extra distance). Go to the next longer club instead of forcing the shot. Grip down on the shaft if necessary to control a shot. Always select a club for control (accuracy means safety) rather than distance.

**Major Problem:** Perfecting the fundamentals—a sound grip, stance and swing. Solve this problem first, and golf will be easier to play. All other problems in the game involve these fundamentals. The correct positions should first be mastered before making alterations.

*A good golf game begins with an understanding of the grip and how important it is in the swing. Learn to hold the club before anything else (opposite page).*

You need a proper understanding of the swing in its entirety before you can hope to play good golf. One way to do this is to break the swing down and study pictures of its different stages. Then you can see how the whole swing fits together and exactly where you should be at each point. This way you'll have a mental picture of what you are doing on the golf course.

## GRIP

All golf begins with the grip. You can quickly master the grip. At first, adjusting to the club may seem strange. There's a good chance that you'll want to grip the shaft your way, a more comfortable way, but if you will take me at my word and hold it the way the pros teach, within an hour and several dozen practice swings, you'll begin to feel at home with the correct grip.

The standard grip is called the overlapping grip. The advantage of the overlapping grip is that the little finger of the right hand overlaps the index finger of the left hand and thus allows the hands to work closely together.

Breaking this grip down, we have the left hand taking hold of the club first. In the left hand we place the club more across the palm and the fingers. This is called the palm-and-finger grip. To test for correct placement (the club should lie underneath the heel of the thumb), place the club in your left hand. Now crook the forefinger. You should be able to pick up the club with just that finger and the heel of the hand. This is your guide point. Once you have the club held this way, simply wrap your other fingers around the shaft, and you will then have your left hand on the club correctly.

The thumb of the left hand slides just to the right-center of the shaft. This creates a V, formed by the thumb and index finger. The V will point between the chin and the right shoulder. Don't have the V too much to the left of the chin or too much to the right of the shoulder if you want a natural grip.

The left-hand pressure points are the last three fingers. Here is where you will hang onto the club at the top and throughout the swing. The left hand must be the dominant force, since it has to lead the club through the swing. Never let the right hand take over during the swing.

When you set the club down, be sure it faces square

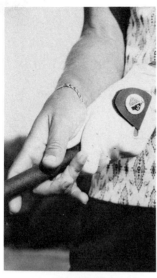

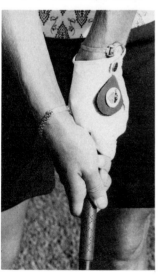

*In a balanced grip, both hands are close together on the shaft. Both Vs should point between the chin and the right shoulder when in place.*

to your line of flight before you take your grip. Never grip your club before you square it up. One easy way to handle this problem is simply to set the club down behind the ball. The shape of the woods will help these clubs to lie naturally; the irons have only to be held in a straight line behind the ball to be in the correct position.

Putting the right hand on the club is simpler if you have the left hand in position first. Put your right hand on the shaft as though you were shaking hands with the club. You have a lifeline under the thumb, and by turning the right thumb in, you create a pocket. Formed by the lifeline and the thumb, this pocket fits over the thumb of the left hand. The right-hand little finger will overlap the left-hand index finger. The hands are then close enough to work together. The pressure points of the right hand are the second and third fingers, with a little pressure from the right thumb. You will hang onto the club with these fingers. The right thumb is to the left-center of the shaft. Again you have a V formed that should point between the chin and the right shoulder. You want these two Vs to be uniform. If your right hand is too far under or over the shaft, it will put you in an unnatural position. (Judy Rankin and other golfers I know who move their left hands far over on the shaft believe that this adjustment is essential for most women golfers. I agree, but you shouldn't try for too extreme an adjustment until you have developed the natural overlapping grip. When you do make the adjustment, see a nearby pro for his assistance.)

A good balanced grip keeps the Vs uniformly pointing between the chin and the right shoulder. If your hands are too far apart on the shaft, they will tend to fight one another, and you'll lose your clubhead speed and the rhythm of your swing. If your grip is correct, the palm of your right hand and the back of your left should face the chin-shoulder target.

*At the address position, Kathy
has a square stance and
is playing the ball off her left
instep. Notice that her left
arm is straight but not stiff.*

## STANCE

The stance is important because you must be in a balanced position at the address. Your weight should be equally distributed on both feet, from the ball of the foot to the heel, without too much weight on the heels or toes. The toes will be pointed slightly outward. This will help you turn, or move your body out of the way of your swing.

The stance used for the driver is the square stance. That is, the left side—including hips, shoulders and feet —are parallel to the line of flight.

Your knees are bent at the address position and throughout the backswing and downswing. By keeping them bent, you are on the same plane and at the same level throughout the swing. The worst thing you can do on your swing is to move your body up, down, back or forth from your address position. You should swing as though your torso were inside a barrel. Bending the knees helps you obtain better balance. You keep them flexed throughout so that when you come back to the ball, you're in the same position you were at the start. If your knees straighten, you'll have a tendency to raise your body, and you'll have to dip to get back down at the ball. This is okay (maybe) if you have great timing, but for the average woman it should be avoided.

If your legs are flexed and moving, you can generate more power, more clubhead speed. This is more important to women than to men, because men are stronger from the waist up, especially in the arms and shoulders. Women's great assets are their legs and hips. They must use these parts of their bodies for power. Keeping the legs flexed throughout the swing will give you better balance while keeping your body at the same level.

When you are standing up to the ball at the address, keep your back fairly straight, but bend slightly from the hips. Many people get the idea it's a waist bend, but actually it is a thrust forward from the hips.

*Women generate power with legs and hips. Legs should be bent for good balance, more power in the golf swing.*

Try to get the feeling that you are about to sit on a stool. This gets the body positioned so that you can turn with a minimum of effort.

To avoid any tendency to reach for the ball or to get too close to the shot, just let the arms hang naturally, and then place the hands on the club, left hand first, with proper palm placement. That way you'll discover how close you should be to the ball. If both feet are balanced on the address, you won't tilt over and reach.

As I have told you, the width of the stance is about the same as the width of the shoulders. If you place

*At the finish, the weight has shifted completely to the left. The width of the stance (opposite page) is the width of the shoulders.*

24

your feet any farther apart than that, you restrict the hip turn. On a full swing such as the driver, you don't want the feet too close; you may lose balance or sway on the shot. I've found that the best results come when the feet are the same width apart as the shoulders.

## SWING

On the weight shift, try to keep your weight just inside the right foot. Once again, the knee flex becomes very important. Your right knee will straighten a little, but by keeping it flexed, you keep the leg from straightening and, as we say, locking the right hip. If your weight is spread too much, you'll tend to lose power as well as to move off the ball. (A tip: You can practice controlling the right side by putting a tee or a ball on the outside of the right foot. This will keep your weight on the inside; it will help to control your motion too.)

Taking the club back, remember: The whole backswing moves together. The shoulder turn, the hip turn and the club are all of one piece. Some golfers say they like to feel the left knee "kicking in." This does not mean that they start to swing with the left knee. The left-knee kick is like a forward press, where you move the hands forward to start the swing back. Anytime you can use some little movement to start your backswing as one piece, fine. But remember that the backswing is a one-piece—not a two- or three-piece—motion. Without this synchronization, your swing "won't work."

The club moves away low to the ground. Some call it "dragging the club back." It's low for about a foot, and then it moves toward the inside. It is merely following the plane of the shoulders. And if you make the proper hip turn, it will throw the club back over your shoulders at the top. Beginners tend to restrict their power by swinging the club first and then their shoulders. If you are in a natural position, the wrists will follow the direction of the arc. Don't worry about them; they will break when they need to. But be care-

*Don't lock the right leg on the weight shift. Keep the legs flexed (above). The club is taken back (opposite page) in a one-piece motion.*

28

ful that the last three fingers of the left hand don't let go.

The move down to the ball from the top begins with the left side moving through first. It's a lateral movement plus a turn, so that you are coming to the ball with the hands leading the clubhead. This is where the term "cocking the hands" comes from. You release the clubhead at the moment of impact, and the hands, leading the clubface, will generate clubhead speed. This happens because you've moved the left side through first. In other words, it's the result of a good downswing. If you have the right grip and a proper swing, the cocking of your wrists will be automatic. The downswing happens so fast, you couldn't possibly think of this motion anyway.

*The club is taken back low to the ground and square (opposite page). The head is kept in one position through the swing, and the left shoulder is tucked under the chin on the turn.*

On the backswing Kathy's left
knee has kicked in, but she has
not lifted her left heel. Her
arms are fully extended.

*At the top of her swing she has*
*shifted most of her weight*
*to the right side, but her*
*position over the ball has not*
*altered at all.*

Follow-through after impact is very important. The follow-through can make up for a "multitude of sins" that you may have committed on the backswing. Even if you've taken the club back too fast or jerked it, a good follow-through can send that ball toward the target and save your shot. But if you stop or slow down during your follow-through because you don't "feel right," you'll spray the ball, compounding any mistakes you've made in the backswing.

It's important to know how to follow through. Most people follow through without knowing what it's all about. As I said, the left side leads the downswing. It leads through until impact, and then the right side, which is actually the power side, takes over. If you're in proper position, you'll be able to follow through with that right side. But never let it take over from the left side until after the impact, when everything is moving naturally up and around toward the finish.

## FAIRWAY WOODS

A fairway wood requires the same square stance as the driver. (I use the square stance more than any other in my golf game.) With a fairway wood, the ball is not played quite so far forward as with a driver. Whereas the driver is played off the toe or instep of the left foot, the fairway wood is played more toward the heel of the left foot.

Most beginners will try to hit the fairway woods on an upswing. This leads to trouble; you sacrifice control over the shot. Try to contact the ball on the downward swing. Don't consciously try to get the ball airborne; let the loft of the club do that for you.

With a very close lie, I'll go with the four-wood instead of the three- just to make sure I get the ball into the air. If you have a five-wood in the bag, use that rather than an iron. The five-wood is a great club to have. Many golfers have difficulty with the long irons. The five-wood solves most of their problems. It

*Notice how Kathy moves her hips out of the way on the downswing (opposite page). She has also shifted her weight to the left side.*

33

*Hands are ahead of the ball at
the address position. On the
downswing (opposite page), the hands
are leading the swing.*

can get the ball up much higher and faster than any long iron, and sometimes better than the four- and five-irons. Judy Rankin swears by it. The club has helped her, as well as many others of us professionals, on the women's tour.

## WOODS FROM THE ROUGH

A wood is often the best club from the long grass because its clubhead slides through grass easier than an iron's. I take my normal square stance and play the ball in the center of my address. My hands, however, move forward, and I have the clubhead aimed toward the right of my target. My reason is that the grass will grab at the clubface when it's coming through and close the face of my club. With this shot I gain a lot of running distance, but not as much carry.

## THE LONG IRONS

With the long irons, the basics—stance and swing—remain the same. You do, however, play the ball more left of center. The hands are slightly ahead of the ball at the address position. On any iron you play, the hands should be slightly forward. You want to contact the ball first, and then the turf. If you hit behind the ball or let your hands drag, you're going to hit the ball heavily, hit behind the ball or catch it thin. You don't, however, hit down. It's more a forward motion than a downward one, with the hands in front of the ball and moving ahead of the club at impact.

If you have a tight lie at the fairway or the rough, go to a club with lots of loft, a five-iron at least. Play the ball back of center and move those hands forward. This will cause you to steepen your swing. Position yourself to the right of the target, because you're likely to hook the shot. You just want to get the clubhead down and through the ball with minimal interference from the grass. Grip the club firmly, because you'll need all your strength on this one.

*These pictures (opposite page) show how steady Kathy's head position is. She looks at the point of impact even after hitting the ball. Notice that her right elbow is kept tight to the body during swing.*

37

*Kathy's right hand takes over*
*only after impact (opposite page).*
*When the swing is completed,*
*all weight has shifted to the left*
*side and she has ended the*
*swing with a high finish.*

*Kathy plays her irons back in the stance (opposite page). Fairway woods and the driver are played off her left instep or toe.*

# THE SHORT IRONS

These are the irons you hit most often. They must be hit with the greatest accuracy. You are hitting them into the green, and you need to get close to the flag. To achieve this accuracy, you need a narrower stance. Since you're not going to take a full swing with any of the short clubs, you won't have a big turn. Sandy Palmer hits the short irons from a square position, as do some of the other women. I am more comfortable playing from an open stance.

Remember that an open stance means drawing the left foot back from the line of flight. Also, open the shoulders and the hips to the shot. This is done to further restrict the swing and give more control. A longer swing could cause you to pull or push the shot. Keep the hands ahead of the ball and contact the ball first. The left side leads through the shot. In fact, the left side dominates these irons more than it does the woods.

Give yourself enough club. Anytime you press the iron, you subject yourself to danger. Occasionally it will work, but only occasionally. If you need more distance, go to a longer club. Never try to hit the short irons farther than a normal swing.

Depending on the shot, I tend to shorten my grip. If the choice is between a nine- and an eight-iron, it's better to choke up and hit with the eight-iron than to push the nine iron. If you're hitting a punch shot, a low shot into the wind, you can grip the club down and play the ball back in the stance.

When I am caught in long grass near the green, I use the wedge. I grip far down the shaft, almost to the leather. With an open, narrow stance, I play the ball well back, off my right foot. Coming off the ball on the backswing, I break my hands immediately and then swing straight back at it. The ball then has a chance to pop out of the tall grass.

With all short iron shots it's important to get

comfortably close to the ball. For the most part, these are soft shots that require not strength but an extraordinary amount of feel or touch. On these shots all of us—men and women—are equal.

## PUTTING

My putting is not based on a normal putting stroke. I use a cut stroke. I take the club back on the outside of the line and cut across the ball. It doesn't work for everyone, but it does work for me, and I can control the ball. To me the main thing in putting is to relax as much as possible. The putting stroke is just a smaller

*In taking the stance, the left foot should turn slightly out. This helps in shifting weight.*

stroke than the big swing. With putting you are working with inches, whereas with the big swing you have more room for error.

In putting, don't do what I do. Try to take the blade straight back and straight through on the line you've decided the ball should travel. The grip is not like that used on the other clubs. It is really the back of the left hand and the palm of the right hand face-to-face on the club and straight up-and-down. They don't turn over, under or on top. This way you don't have the tendency to close the clubface or open it when you take the putter back. You have what we call a pendulum-type stroke, a free-swinging stroke.

*Kathy does not sway off the ball on the backswing (opposite page), nor does her head move. In gripping the putter, hands should come together on the club like a handshake.*

There are several kinds of basic putting strokes. There's the wrist stroke, the combination-of-wrist-and-arms stroke, the strictly arms-and-shoulders stroke. All of them can be effective. I've seen good putters use all types. Whatever is comfortable for you is what you should use. Putting is very individual. Some golfers use a wide stance, others a very narrow one. Some squat, others stand straight. Some put their knees together until they look like contortionists. It doesn't matter.

The only basic rule about ball position in putting is that if you have a fairly normal stance and the weight is on your left side, you should play the ball toward your left side. If you play the ball toward your right side, you should always put your weight toward your right side.

Regardless of what stance you use, you want to keep your eyes over the ball. If your eyes fall behind the ball, between the ball and your feet, then you are looking at the line of putt from an angle. You're not looking straight down, and therefore your line will be wrong. The same thing happens if you're too far over the ball. From that side you'll most likely pull the ball.

One thing I try to do in my putting is to keep the club moving straight through to the target. Again, the follow-through is important. Regardless of what you do on the backswing, if you get the putter through the ball and can "feel" the ball toward the hole, you've a good chance of dropping the putt. It's your natural sense of direction. If I'm having a poor day, I fall back on my sense of feel.

It is important also to remain steady over the ball. Try to visualize the shot and know the line. Then concentrate on the ball. This will keep you steady, keep you from moving off the ball. It really works. But remember: Concentrate all the way through the stroke, not just at the beginning.

I don't worry about the stroke while I'm on the green. You may make a perfect stroke but forget to hit

*Kathy putts the ball off the left toe. She does not break her wrists on the stroke. Note how long clubhead is kept on backstroke and follow-through.*

*Make sure your eyes are over the ball. Check alignment the way Kathy checks her position.*

*Stay steady over the ball even
after striking the putt.*

49

the ball. Putting is feel! Only through a great deal of practice do you become a good putter. You must develop your sense of feel. Only you, for example, know how far you should take the putter back on each putt. And only by trying to make a lot of putts from a lot of different positions can you learn how to hit those putts.

Feel can carry you a long way on the green, but you must have the basic information down: a correct grip, palm facing palm; a putter blade that is square; head and eyes directly over the ball and putter; a steady comfortable stance and knowledge of the line to the hole.

## POINTS TO REMEMBER

1. The golf swing begins with a sound grip and a square stance. Learn these two aspects of the swing first.

2. A good swing requires that you pivot off the left leg and transfer weight to your right side before beginning the downswing.

3. The downswing begins with a lateral movement toward the left side, and then the hip turn.

4. Complete every swing. A good follow-through can make up for errors committed on the backswing.

5. Fairway woods should be hit on the downswing, not the upswing.

6. On long irons, the hands should be slightly ahead of the ball at the address position.

7. When putting, be certain that you are standing with your eyes directly over the ball.

On the follow-through,
stay down and finish in one motion.
Never stop on the swing.

Kathy Whitworth, who plays all
shots from tee to green with great
skill, is the dominant
figure on the women's tour.

# Betty Burfeindt

# Driving for Distance

Betty Burfeindt had her best year on the LPGA Tour in 1972, winning over $47,000 and two tournaments: the Birmingham Centennial and the Sealy Classic. At 5 feet 4 inches and only 114 pounds, Betty is one of the longest hitters on the pro tour. From Canaan, New York, she graduated from Cortland State University. She taught physical education for several years before turning professional in 1969. During the 1972 winter Betty spent six months working with Johnny Revolta to improve her game. She credits her wins on the circuit to this instruction. Her advice on the driver can help you.

**Grip:** I advise a strong left-hand grip on the club with hands snugly together. Both Vs should point to the right shoulder.

**Stance:** Wide as the shoulders with toes of both feet pointing out. Weight is distributed evenly. Left leg is forward in a closed position to the line of flight.

**Swing:** Club is taken back in a one-piece motion with the left arm fully extended. At the top of the swing, club reaches a parallel position. Club is pulled back on the downswing by the left arm.

**Club Selection:** Important to have weight and shaft that are correct for your type of swing. Have the swing weight and the length checked by a professional.

**Major Problem:** Obtaining enough pivot and shoulder turn to generate clubhead speed without losing the club at the top of the swing.

As with the other clubs in the bag, you're not going to get very far with the driver unless the basic elements of your golf game are correct. The driver is a long and heavy club to use. The address position is the first element of concern.

I use a slightly closed stance, as do most women on the tour. The closed position is the best for distance. The ball is played off my left instep. Some women stretch a bit and place the ball off the left toe, but the instep works best for me. I have both feet turned slightly out. This helps me a great deal on my pivot and aids in getting the hip out of the way on the downswing.

I have what is called a strong left arm setup. It appears that I am tense at the ball, but actually I'm not. I'm very comfortable, with my legs flexed and my back almost straight. I don't bend over the driver. This makes it difficult to turn properly with such a long-shafted club.

*When driving, Betty uses a closed stance with a straight left arm. Notice the strong left-hand grip she employs.*

The driver is taken back
(opposite page) and away in
one motion. The left knee
kicks into the turn.
Betty has a big shoulder turn
with her swing. Notice the
position of her left shoulder
at the top of the swing.

I take the club back low to the ground with the left arm fully extended. My left shoulder and my left hip turn with the backswing, and as my left knee kicks in, the weight shifts over to the right side of my body. I don't, however, lock that right side, as it takes the balance of my weight. Notice that the right leg is still flexed. Also, I haven't pulled off the shot. My head is directly over the ball. At the top of the swing, my left shoulder is fully tucked under my chin. This allows my club to get up and over the top into a parallel position. The clubhead doesn't drop any farther than that. If it did, I would lose control of the swing. Other golfers— Sandy Haynie, for instance—can control that club beyond the parallel position. Don't try it.

At the top of the swing I am in as tight a coil as possible. And I have to achieve this without swaying off the ball. If you study the pictures, you will notice that I haven't moved my head and certainly haven't moved my eyes. They are riveted to that ball. Keeping my head steady ensures that I pivot in one position.

Coming back to the ball, I start the action with the left arm pulling the clubhead down and around. My left hip moves out of the way immediately, my left heel has replaced itself and I'm driving into my left side. But it's not a blocked left side. I am free to move my weight and my right side into a powerful finish. The left side also isn't locked. My left knee is still flexed, and it stays that way until impact.

On the downswing, the right arm plays a much more important role. I am conscious of throwing my right hand and arm into the swing and gaining all the power I can. At the point of impact I have cleared my left hip out of the way, and my whole left side, from the shoulder blade, arm and back of my left hand, is square to the target. My hands are in exactly the same position as they were at the address.

At impact I have everything I own driving into the ball. My right side is pulled off the ground, and I keep swinging out, letting the club follow the ball off

*The club is parallel to the ground at top of the swing and is completely under control (opposite page).*

On downswing hips move out of
the way first. Betty's powerful swing carries her to a
high finish with the woods.

the tee. Notice how the speed of the clubhead has pulled my body around, though even after impact my head has kept its position. It is only when my hands are about shoulder high that I look to follow the flight of the ball. I have a very high finish, and the club is extended as far as my arms will allow. I haven't, however, fallen off the ball. The position of my body is still within the width of my stance. My weight has transferred back completely to my left side.

What you really want to achieve with the driver is clubhead speed, so that at the point of impact, you have all your power going for you. You can't swing softly at the ball and obtain distance. Your swing should gradually build up speed through the backswing, and then coil but not stop at the top. If the swing stops at the top, you'll lose that momentum created on the backswing. Think of having your swing go against a bank at the top. Then move off that bank as if you were rounding a tight corner with your car, and let the clubhead continue to gain speed on the downswing and right through the ball. Keep the momentum moving beyond the point of impact.

With so much acceleration on the swing, there is a tendency to raise up off the ball. You have to keep yourself solid in the stance. By leaning forward or raising up, you'll get outside the line of flight and cut across the ball, causing a slice. Keep down and keep back on this swing. Notice where my head is at the point of impact. I'm slightly behind the ball, making sure my weight is pushing the shot.

It is necessary for women to get off the tee with good distance. Otherwise we are just not going to score well in courses with long yardages. In most of the courses I've played, scoring is a problem. But I think that it is possible for us to drive with the men. I have noticed that more and more of the women professionals are driving the ball 240 and 250 yards off the tees. We have power—especially in the legs and arms—that can drive the ball, but you are not going to get that power

*Pictures on pages 64 and 65 (following) show the strength of Betty's swing and her ability to get the power of hips and legs into her golf swing.*

IN GOLF WE TRUST

# goofy golfin

WHICH IS MORE EXCITING? WATCHING GOLFERS GOLF OR WATCHING GRASS GROW? YOU SAY, PROBABLY THE LATTER? SOUNDS LIKE A GOOD CHOICE!

HERE'S AN EXCITING GOLF STORY -

There were two amateur golfers, one was Jack and the other was Arnie. One nice morning they set out to the Gold'n Bare Cuntree Club in Palmer Springs, CA (home of the St.Nicholas Open). Jack teed off and the ball went so high it hit a birdie and the birdie came tumbling down to earth to its sudden death. Then as Jack and Arnie approached the birdie, to their great surprise, it jumped up and started to bogey (I mean boogie), then one of them noticed something about its wing, it had a hole in one. Apparently made by the golf ball. As they approached even closer the birdie suddenly takes off soaring off like an eagle, never to be seen again. So stunned were the pair of amateur golfers that they couldn't concentrate and ended up finishing their game incident that they couldn't concentrate and ended up finishing their game more than two dozen strokes over par. So what did they do then? They headed back to the club house and spent the rest of the day in the bar. Of course, no one there believed their birdie story and thought they were nuts. They became very teed off and left. And that's the end of the story.

NOW WASN'T THAT AN EXCITING STORY?

with a soft swing and little turn of the hips and shoulders. You need to increase the rate of the body turn and the power of the clubhead moving into the ball. I firmly believe that you can do it by lengthening your swing to its maximum and by developing a good pivot. Any woman can increase her drives off the tee by twenty yards if she works at it. Caution: Don't speed up the backswing to get more distance. That is a sure way to lose hitting power. It is the body turn, the coiling of the body and the weight release that generate power.

*Betty is fully extended at all points of her swing. Full extension creates a bigger arc and that means longer drives.*

# POINTS TO REMEMBER

1. Play the ball off the left instep. The driver is played the farthest forward of all clubs. The stance is square.

2. Use a one-piece motion with a long, extended arc. The club is taken back low to the ground to generate that wide arc.

3. The weight shifts around the head, and the club reaches a parallel position at the top of the swing.

4. The downswing begins with a pulling action of the left hand.

5. Build clubhead speed by a full turn of the shoulders and a large pivot. This increases the overall swinging arc.

6. The left hip turns out of the way on the downswing. The left shoulder also opens up.

7. Keep the head down even after the point of impact. Let the speed of the clubhead through the shot pull you around to a finish.

*Although Betty is very small, she is able to drive the ball by using all the strength of her body. These two pictures show the force of her swing through impact and into a high, controlled finish.*

68

# Judy Rankin

# Playing the Woods from Fairway and Rough

Judy Rankin is one of the tiniest players on the LPGA Tour, standing 5 feet 3 inches and weighing just 110 pounds. She started to play golf at the age of six. She turned professional in 1962 at 17, one of the youngest players ever to join the tour. She is also one of the few married players on the tour. Her husband and young son follow her on the circuit.

In 1972 Judy won the Lady Eve Open. Altogether, she has won seven events and is eleventh on the official winning list, with over $158,000 in prize money. Petiteness to the contrary, she is one of the more powerful swingers among the women professionals, especially with her woods.

**Grip:** Keep a strong left hand over the top of the shaft, with four knuckles showing, and a normal right-hand grip.

**Stance:** Ball is played off the inside of the left foot on fairway shots. The stance is square or slightly closed. In the rough the ball is positioned back toward center, and the stance is open.

**Swing:** A big extension and a sweeping motion that drives down and through the ball, as on the drive. In the rough the wrists break sooner than on a normal swing. The club is taken back along the line.

**Club Selection:** The five-wood is the most useful club for the rough. For the fairway it should replace the two-iron. The wood is more versatile.

**Major Problem:** Generating enough clubhead speed to get through long grass in the rough or to achieve distance on the fairway.

Because the woods have such long shafts, they appear to baffle some women. But I'm only 5 feet 3 inches and I can handle them. So I'm convinced that any woman can play the woods well.

Because of the length of wood clubs, women tend to set themselves up too far from the ball. They reach unnecessarily, and this causes them to tense—particularly in the left side. They then jerk the left arm into a locked position and never give themselves a chance to swing at the ball.

If you begin by letting your arms hang naturally and then assume the stance, you'll find yourself the correct distance from the ball, with enough space to make the proper turn. Perhaps the biggest fault women golfers have is that they aren't the correct distance from the ball. They are either too far away or too close, and they block themselves when swinging.

To swing the woods correctly, as with any club in the bag, you must depend a good deal on what we call *tempo*. The whole swing is really a piece of art. It has its own dimensions, its own aesthetics. A smooth, steady swing is a thing of beauty. I think all of us receive pleasure from just watching someone like Sam Snead with a fine swing play golf.

Once you discover your own tempo—and there is nothing mysterious about it—you'll play much better. Tempo is as natural to a person as rhythm. What you must do is to build your swing inside that rhythm. This will ensure that you never lose control of the club. The clubhead then builds up speed through the swing, so that you will hit the ball with your maximum power.

There are differences between playing the woods from the fairway and from the rough, and any woman who wants to play well should understand them.

## PLAYING FROM THE FAIRWAY

Normally with the fairway woods, you want to use the three-wood and play the ball from inside the left foot. The stance should be square or slightly closed. With this stance you'll achieve more distance on the ball. The fairway wood is hit with basically the same stroke as the driver. You should try for a big extension going back. Usually you should strive to hit the three-wood all-out.

The swing begins with taking the club away from the ball in one piece. If you have made the extension big enough on the backswing, you'll get more distance. In my own swing I know I hit the ball 20 to 30 yards farther with a long extension.

Swing the club back low in a fairly flat plane, and at the top of the swing try to be parallel. I believe in the flat plane because I don't want to swing upright with my small build. I feel I lose too much strength swinging upright. I can get a bigger arc and a longer extension by swinging the club flat.

*Ball is played from the rough with a closed stance. Notice (opposite page) how Judy moves the right hip back on the shift of her weight.*

These pictures show the low or
flat plane of Judy's swing.
This swing gives her a longer
arc and greater clubhead speed.

It is equally important to use your legs well on the woods. As you take the club back, shift your weight to the right side. On my swing, the shift of weight is quite visible. From the top, the first move is to start my left foot in motion. In other words, I start the lower part of my body before the upper. So on your swing, let the lower part of your body be the leader and the top part follow. This way, at impact you can feel you are getting everything behind the ball. All your power is saved for impact if nothing is released at the top of the swing.

My concern in beginning the swing and moving away from the ball is to have a fully extended left arm. I don't mean a stiff left arm. When the club gets just about waist high, my hands begin to break. My weight has shifted somewhat to my right side, and it continues to move until I get to the top. My first move at the top is to replace the left heel. On the backswing, that left heel has come off the ground about four inches. By replacing the left heel first, I get the lower part of my body moving. It makes for the small lateral move inherent in the swing. That's the reason you shift your weight in the first place; otherwise you could just spin on the ball. But then you wouldn't have power, and you couldn't direct your swing.

The upper part of the body begins to move with the turn of the shoulders. Since they have started later, they are behind the clubhead. The clubhead is meeting the ball almost in a sweep, as you'd hit a driver off the tee. What you must do with a wood is to hit that ball flush. You get maximum distance with this kind of position at the ball. It won't work, however, if the ball isn't sitting well in the grass.

The distance that the ball is driven on any shot is determined by the speed and weight of the clubhead. I think that with my swing—a big arc and a flat plane —I generate maximum speed with the clubhead at impact. I don't lift the ball off this lie, but sweep the clubhead through the shot, and that way I generate speed. I could hit down and through with the three-

*The lower part of Judy's body controls the swing. Her right knee breaks forward as her downswing begins.*

*These three pictures show how Judy generates power in her swing. Note that her right elbow is well tucked in.*

wood, but I wouldn't hit the ball as far that way, and I wouldn't have the same flowing motion. I differ slightly with Kathy Whitworth on this approach to the woods. Now I do hit down and through an iron, but with an iron distance isn't that much of a factor.

Some women play this shot off the fairway with a two-wood. For a while I used the two-wood, but it's a difficult club to use, and I've found that I can get more and better use from the five-wood.

## UPHILL LIE

With an uphill lie in the fairway, you want to play the ball slightly forward. You want the feeling that you are swinging the club on the contour of the ground. I find that on an uphill lie, it helps a lot to try not to shift my

*With uphill lies play the woods off the left heel, the weight somewhat to the right side.*

weight too much to my right. If I get my stance, if I try to stay there and hit the ball mainly with my arms and hands, I am better off. If I shift the weight to my right side and the hill is steep, I'm lost, and I can't get back to the ball. But if I leave my weight centered, it's a lot easier to hit the ball flush. If the ball is considerably above me, I will move down an inch or so on the club to obtain better leverage on the shot.

The major points to remember for uphill lies are moving the ball forward in the stance, playing it off the left toe, keeping the weight shift to a minimum, choking up if the lie is severe and trying to swing at the ball with the contour of the land. On an uphill lie the natural tendency is to hook or draw the ball, so aim more to the right and let the ball draw itself toward the target.

If the uphill lie isn't particularly severe, you won't make all these adjustments. But you will aim the ball a bit farther right and let the shot have a few extra yards to draw toward the target.

## DOWNHILL LIE

On downhill lies it will be necessary to play the ball back in the stance. Depending on the severity of the hill, the ball could be positioned past the center. You should be aware that on a downhill lie the ball will move from left to right. Swinging the club on this contour of the ground, you will find it difficult to release the hands and hit the ball straight. I find that on a severe downhill lie the shot becomes a lot easier if I swing the club a bit up on the outside and, again as in the rough, break my hands a bit faster. It makes it easier to come down and hit the ball first rather than the hill.

I think about making good contact with the ball, hitting it flush and staying down with it while keeping the club moving always toward the target. Someone told me long ago—and I thought it was very well put

—that the longer the club travels toward the target, the longer the ball will go straight. And it's true.

Another point to remember: If the lie is so bad that you have to change your stance, you should also change your club—for a wood or iron with more loft.

I hit the severe downhill lies the same way I hit the ball out of a bad lie in the rough. The idea is the same. Concentrate fully on hitting the ball first.

## HOOK AND SLICE

At times from these lies it will be necessary to hook the ball or draw it or slice the shot. It may be a lot

*Ball is played well back on downhill lies (opposite page). Hands are forward and down a few inches on the shaft. Knees are flexed.*

*Judy Rankin plays with a very strong left-hand grip (above). It's well over on the shaft. Playing from the rough (opposite page), move the ball back in the stance and break the wrists sooner to pick the clubhead out of the long grass.*

easier to play the ball this way, depending on the slope of the ground.

On the hook make just two adjustments. Move the left hand over on the shaft so that it is on top of the club, and then close the stance slightly. On uphill lies making the hook work is a simple proposition.

For the slice you just reverse the order. The right hand on the shaft is now dominant, and the stance is open, with the left foot back off the line of the flight. A slice is natural off a downhill lie.

## IN THE ROUGH

In the rough I would rarely use a three-wood. Normally I swing a four-wood or a five-wood, depending on the lie. I play the ball slightly further back than normal, but still a little ahead of the center of my stance, to make absolutely sure that the clubhead will meet the ball first in order to get up and out.

In the rough, when I have moved the ball back in my stance, I break my hand away from the ball a little sooner. That's another way to make sure I hit the ball first and not the turf. And breaking my hands quickly makes the ball pop up a little higher from deep grass.

I didn't carry a five-wood in my bag until four or five years ago. I carried the two-iron, but I'm now a great believer in the five-wood. For women, it is a better club to have. I can do things with a five-wood I never could do with a two-iron. I get more distance, and I can stop the ball better. I can hit it out of almost any kind of lie. If I want to hit it a little shorter, I just move my hands down on the shaft and take a normal swing. For my money, it's a much easier club to use in every way.

If the ball is sitting up high in the rough, however, I wouldn't use the five-wood. I would try the four- or the three-wood to keep the clubhead from slipping under the ball. On an exceptionally good lie from the rough, out of long, course grass, the ball will run, and you have to take into consideration that you might go over the green with a longer club.

In the rough, I think that women are at a disadvantage. This is one of the few places on a golf course where they are. Brute strength often is the sole requirement for getting out of long grass, and few women have that kind of strength.

When I have moved the ball back toward center, I also open my stance just a bit. I want to get the feeling that I am cutting the ball, swinging the club across the line of flight instead of inside/outside the line of flight. When I have moved the ball back and opened my stance to the line of flight, my hands are now slightly forward on the shot. But when the lie is tight, you must keep your hands forward in order to get the ball.

Starting the club back, I break my wrists sooner than normal while taking the hands just outside the line. My first move on the top of the swing is to pull down in an effort to hit the ball first and go through the shot. You must get through the ball, regardless of the lie or length of the rough.

My left hand is over on the grip quite a bit. I strongly believe in this kind of grip for a woman. It makes the game a lot easier for them and provides additional strength. The key to this grip is to keep the clubhead moving through the shot. If I let up, I will hook the ball. At times I might block the shot, but usually this indicates that I haven't released the hands, not that my left hand is over the top of the grip.

I don't see many women playing with this strong left-handed grip, but if I were starting someone out in golf, I'd teach them that grip. It makes up for much of what we lack in strength.

One last point. The woods can be played well from the fairway and the rough. It takes time and attention and determination, but they are clubs to be used.

*This picture series shows the shift in leg positions. Left knee goes to right. Judy is at the top of her swing (below left). Right knee goes left as downswing accelerates to the ball (below right).*

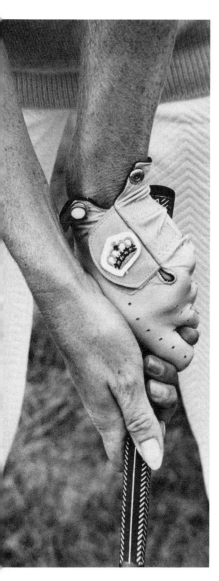

*Note strong left-hand grip
(above), firmness of right
and overlap. Note Judy's
big hip turn on woods (opposite).*

# POINTS TO REMEMBER

1. Develop a swing that is natural to your tempo, but always in control.

2. Keep the backswing low and in the largest possible arc to generate clubhead speed at impact.

3. On the downswing the lower part of the body moves first, followed by the shoulders and arms.

4. Hit down and through all wood shots. Never quit on the club in the rough.

5. Swing with the contour of the land, and let the lie help you make the shot.

6. In the rough play the ball back and stand slightly open to the line of flight.

*From the rough, Judy gets additional power by using a strong left-hand grip, a quick club pickup (below) and by pulling a strong left arm through the shot (opposite).*

7. Always finish the shot in the rough. The clubhead can be pulled through on the downswing with a strong left arm leading the swing.

# Sandy Haynie

# Playing the Long Irons to Score

Born in Ft. Worth, Texas, in 1943, Sandra Haynie has been a professional for 12 years. A scant 5 feet 5 inches and 120 pounds, she owns one of the finest swings on the tour. This blue-eyed blonde has had an impressive career as a professional. She has already won 26 tournaments, and she is ranked fifth on the all-time money-winning list. She has won over $265,000 in official earnings. In 1970 she was voted LPGA Professional of the Year. In 1971 she won four tournaments, including the Dallas Civitan and the San Antonio Open. In 1972 she won three tournaments and over $39,000 in prize money. Sandy is one of the best long-iron players among the women. This chapter illustrates why.

**Grip:** Use a strong left- and right-hand grip, with both hands over the top of the shaft. The club is taken back square from the ball.

**Stance:** A square stance with the ball forward, off the left instep. Weight is centered and back on the heels. Feet are wider apart than the shoulders at the address.

**Swing:** Wrist break immediately. Club is taken farther back than normal, past the parallel line. Shot is hit with a sweeping motion, not on the descending arc.

**Club Selection:** Long irons are difficult clubs to play unless the woman is particularly strong. Might be better off hitting a five-wood instead of a two-iron on most shots.

**Major Problem:** Overcoming the tendency to try lifting the ball off the ground instead of taking an extended arc and sweeping through on the long irons. Natural loft of the club will get the ball into the air.

Begin your play with a little warm-up session; it's invaluable. Every day you'll discover, when you tee up the ball, that you're hitting the clubs a little differently. You need to know that before going out on the course. Don't hit a lot of balls, just enough to loosen up and discover how you're playing. This brief warm-up refreshes the muscle memory, too, and that's necessary for your swing.

When you get out on the course and need to play a long iron, it is important to remember a few basic points before addressing the ball. Perhaps the major point is that you don't have to lift the ball off the turf with these irons. Women see the small face of the two- or three-iron, and they think the club needs help getting the shot away. The club, however, is made for the purpose of hitting a longer and a lower shot. Just keep in mind that you want to hit the shot. The club will take care of itself.

*No turf is taken on the long irons. Ball is played forward off a square stance (opposite page).*

Start by getting a good stance. The ball is played off the left heel. Keep the ball forward in the stance, so that at contact the natural loft of the club gets the ball off the ground. You don't have to force this loft. Many people have a tendency to flip their hands when they are making contact. It isn't necessary, and it takes away power.

Also, don't hit down on the shot. The long irons are sweep shots, clean shots with a little turf. It's more a matter of hitting the ball first. You'll make a small divot, but you will not be hitting down at the ball, as with your shorter irons. Hit the longer irons as you would the four- and five-wood. The swing is the same.

I hit my long irons with the same swing I use for most of my shots. It's important to keep the same tempo in your golf game, whether you are making a chip shot or a drive. Everything functions the same. If you try to change your swing as you go from short irons to long irons to woods, you will ruin your game. Golf is difficult enough without having to think about a different swing for each shot.

Once again, the most important things are good stance and good grip. Without these two parts of the game, you're lost. After them come good timing and good balance. If you have these four parts of your swing under control, you'll do all right.

I address all shots pretty much the same, and I play the ball forward for all shots. I don't have a big move going back to the right side, and I don't shift a lot of weight. Everything in my golf game revolves around my left side, so I concentrate my efforts there.

I start with a square stance, with the ball forward, and try to get the weight centered and back on my heels. My first move is one which not every gal pro employs. I immediately break my wrists. Most people start the club back and break the wrists naturally, about waist-high. But when I started playing, breaking my wrists immediately was just something I did. So I preferred to stay with it as I progressed in my game.

*These pictures illustrate the complete wrist movement of Sandy's swing. Notice how close both hands are on the grip.*

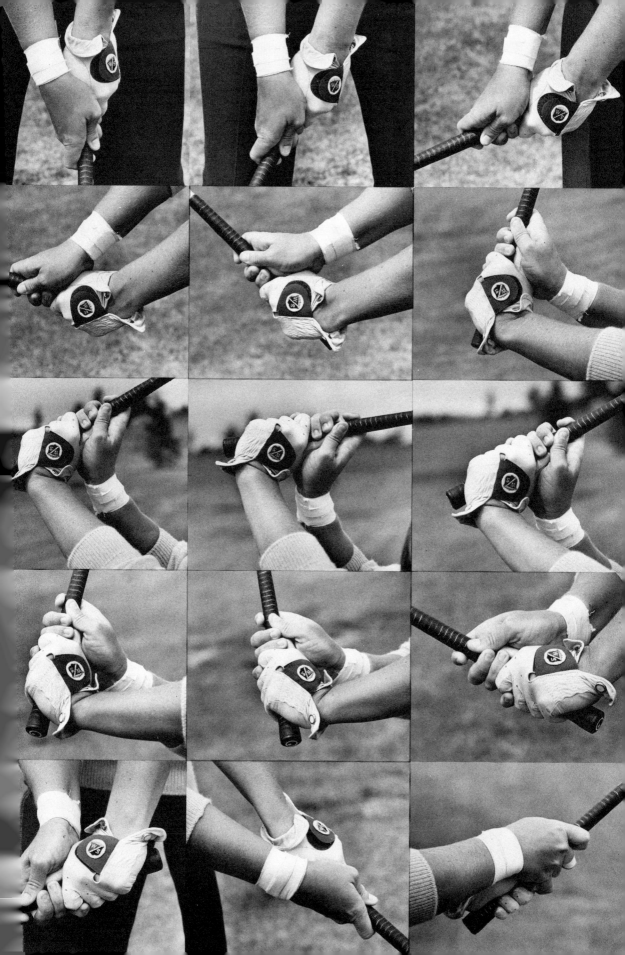

For me it's a simple move, but certainly not one for you to experiment with.

Taking the club back, I go further than the parallel line. I think women have to do this. We have to have a longer club, a bigger swing and a bigger turn to generate power. We need all the power we can get to hit long irons. That's why they are the most difficult clubs in the bag to do well with. That's also why we have some women on the professioial tour who use five- and even six-woods. They use those woods like magic wands and don't even carry the two- and three-irons. We also have some women who carry one-irons in

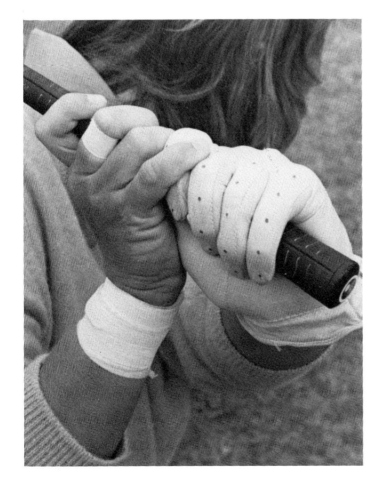

*In these two pictures, notice the swing plane that Sandy employs, her straight left arm (opposite page) and her grip control at the top.*

*Sandy achieves a full shoulder*
*turn with her high-plane swing.*

their bags. Whether you can hit the irons or not, really depends on your particular golf game.

I think I am a strong iron player. I can hit them pretty well. Many times I'd rather hit the two-iron than a wood. I can control a two-iron better. But being small, I still have to do everything I can to generate power. I have a big shoulder turn, and that helps the clubhead speed. The bigger the arc, as others have said in this book, the more power you'll be able to achieve.

In any woman's game, she is going to need a big turn and what looks like a lot of movement in order to get clubhead speed. Unfortunately, we are generally not strong enough to get power with a small turn and a short backswing.

My legs, for example, are turning about 45 degrees, and the top of my body is turning perhaps 90 degrees and maybe a bit more. This great division between the top and the bottom of the swing is what causes the coil. I don't shift a lot of weight, but I still get coil.

In a normal golf swing, when the wrists break waist-high, you probably will shift a little more weight from the left side to the right side and back again on the shot. You will get more lateral movement in this type of golf swing than I do with mine. Mine is mainly a tight coil with little weight shift.

With either one of these turning actions, you need a solid foundation for the long irons. The big golf swing demands that the stance be slightly wider than normal. But you have to be comfortable on the turn. The bigger the swing, the bigger the stance. I turn out my left foot slightly for the big swing, though usually I play with both feet square.

All golfers—men and women—have heard a lot of talk about the square-to-square method. Square-to-square is pretty much the way I play. It is very difficult to learn once you have learned another method. It is particularly difficult for women, because they need to be strong in the wrists and hands just to hold the clubs in this position. For someone starting golf it is probably

*On her swing Sandy keeps her*
*weight evenly distributed.*

*Sandy plays with a square-to-square swing. The club is closed on the backswing.*

the simplest way to learn, but I can't really recommend it for anyone who's been at the game for a while. It is not the most natural way to swing.

If you take up a broom and sweep, your hands will rotate: open, square and closed. This is a natural golf swing. It is the way your arms move. Now in square-to-square, the club is immediately put into a square position and held throughout the entire golf swing. That is very hard for most women to achieve.

When you are hitting the long irons into the green —and that happens often—you must make several considerations before playing the shot. The long iron, as you know, will roll, and it is hard to control. You have to know how far you will carry the ball and what kind of green you're playing. Is it deep? Shallow? If you are going into a shallow green, you'll want to hit the ball a little higher in order to hold the ball.

The first thing I do is to decide how many yards I have to the green and whether I should let the ball carry all the way or land short and run up to the flag. Usually it is easier to play short and let the ball run.

I play all my shots with a little draw. That is, I hit the ball from right to left. I have a natural draw motion with my swing. It's caused by the club moving inside/out and the clubface being closed just a bit at impact. Everyone has a natural move. I suggest you discover what yours is and build it into your swing.

Women should experiment with their abilities. I don't see enough of that happening. But find out *your* abilities, not your friend's. We are all built differently, and therefore our individual swings require adjustments from what we might call a perfect swing. Few of us have perfect swings.

For example, in the normal stance, your feet are as far apart as your shoulders, but some women have very narrow shoulders, or short legs, and that has to be taken into consideration. You have to experiment to find out what is right for you. I may swing a C-9 club, but there are several women on the tour who are too strong for a club as light as C-9. There are also women who should be swinging a C-6 or a C-5, and they'll say that's too light because their best friend swings a C-9. It doesn't matter what your friend swings. Get the weight and shaft that are right for you and play your own game.

## POINTS TO REMEMBER

1. Be sure that your fundamentals are sound. Have a good grip, stance and swing.

2. The long irons should be hit with a sweeping motion, not on a descending arc. The ball should be hit, not picked off the turf.

3. Long irons require a bigger turn and arc, as well as a wider stance, to generate enough power to get the ball off the ground and into the air.

4. The square-to-square method should be used only by women who are naturally strong in the wrists and arms. For most women it is not a good method.

5. With a long iron the ball will roll a great deal. Know where you want the ball to land before hitting into the green.

6. Hit the long irons as you would the four- and five-woods.

7. Not all women can hit long irons. Your swing may require a five- or six-wood instead. Don't worry if you can't play those difficult long irons.

# Sandy Palmer
# Playing the Short Irons

At 5 feet 2 inches, Sandy Palmer is one of the best shotmakers on the tour. Born in 1941, she has lived all her life in Ft. Worth, Texas. Sandy started playing golf at 13, when she caddied on her summer vacation in Bangor, Maine. She turned professional in 1964 after graduating from North Texas State University.

In 1971 Sandy won both the Sealy Classic and the Heritage Open. In 1972 she won the Titleholders Championship and, with Jane Blalock, the Angelo's LPGA 4-ball. To date she has won over $144,000.

Here Sandy talks about the critical short irons, the stroke savers. They are clubs she uses very well indeed.

*Sandy shows (upper picture) how the club can get away at the top of the swing, and (next) the proper control. Sandy shows (opposite page) where to hold the club in the left hand.*

**Grip:** It is important that the hands hold tightly to the club at all times and in all parts of the swing.

**Stance:** Play the short irons from a square stance. The left toe flares out, but the right foot is perpendicular to the line of flight. This square right foot helps establish tension on the back swing.

**Swing:** Three-quarter backswing at the most. Hands are played forward at the address to enable the ball to be struck before the turf. Left arm is kept straight, but not locked, throughout the swing.

**Club Selection:** Know how much distance you can obtain from each of the short irons. Don't force the club beyond what it (or you) can manage. Try to hit each club the same distance every time.

**Major Problem:** Achieving perfect alignment with the short irons. Check continually to see that your stance is correct. Do this by placing a club by your feet along the intended line of flight.

I think that the key to golf is consistency. To be consistent, a golfer must make her every swing fundamentally sound, whether it is with the driver or with the short irons. Therefore, the basic parts of the swing must be understood and practiced by any woman who expects to play good golf. And the most elementary part of the golf swing is the grip. I know that Kathy Whitworth has gone into detail about the grip, but here are a few points that pertain to the short irons.

## GRIP

I have small hands, and this presents problems. It's a little harder for us to hold onto the club. But if we don't hang onto the club with a firm grip, we'll let the club loose at the top of the swing and lose most of our power there.

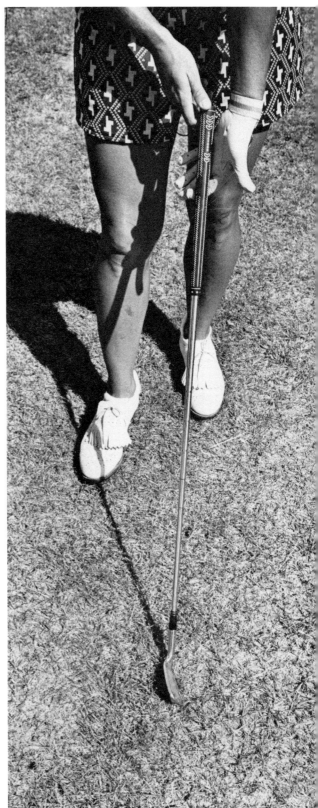

I hold the club diagonally across the left fingers and under the pad of flesh at the heel of my left hand. I hold it firmly with the last three fingers of the left hand and the thumb and the forefinger of the right hand. The guide for my swing is the left hand, and the power is the right hand. I try to vary my grip according to what shot I'm going to hit. I don't think you should play from the same grip all the time. This view is different from those of many women on the tour; they adjust their stance for a draw or a slice. I turn my left hand over on top, for example, if I'm going to draw the ball, or I have a weak left-hand grip if I want to slice the shot.

*Sandy uses both a yardstick and an iron to check position and direction she is facing.*

## ADDRESS

Once I am secure and comfortable with my grip, I make my address. I merely drop the club to the ground, and my distance from the ball is determined by the length of the club. I keep myself from reaching for the ball by slightly flexing the knees. My back is kept fairly straight, and I make sure that my weight is balanced between both feet. When I am in this position, my left arm is firm but not locked. Ideally, the left arm is straight at the address and straight at the top of the swing, and it remains straight all the way down and through the ball. By maintaining a straight left arm, you have a fuller extension through the shot and a greater arc. A wider arc is needed—especially for women—to generate more clubhead speed.

At my address, I have positioned the ball forward of center. I play all my shots—whether with an eight-iron or the three-wood—from this same position. I be-

lieve that most women have to do this, because it increases the arc of the swing, giving us more time to release the club.

On the shorter irons I also play the ball from a square stance. My right foot is perpendicular to the line of flight. The reason for my square right foot is very important. I need a tight wind on my swing. I swing all my weight into that firm right leg. It coils there, helping me to release my strength on the downswing. I place the left foot with a slight flare. This enables me to turn through the shot and to keep my hips out of the way on the follow-through. My hands are placed ahead of the ball at the address position. I think that all good iron shots are hit this way. It's important to catch the ball first and the turf second; that is, catch the ball on a descending arc.

The short-iron swing need never be more than three-quarters. Since you are striving for accuracy and

*Sandy plays from a square stance with her hands forward. On her backswing she moves her weight to the right side.*

115

control with these irons, distance isn't that much of a consideration. Everyone should know exactly how far they can hit the seven-, eight- or nine-iron and be content with that distance. Don't try to stretch the iron. Just use the next longer club.

The swing itself is a one-piece motion of the clubhead, hands, arms and shoulders, with the whole left side moving at one time. The weight shifts to the right side, brakes against the right foot and then shifts left once again. Don't use one swing for the longer irons and another swing for the short clubs. Use the same swing for all clubs. It's important for consistency.

With women, especially the average woman golfer, getting the ball into the air is a problem. The reason women have trouble getting the ball up is that they do not have much speed through the ball. They do not accelerate on their shots. Each of us can only accelerate so much. We can achieve only so much clubhead speed, so it is important to obtain maximum power on all our shots. We accomplish this by doing two simple things.

## ACCELERATION

Achieve maximum acceleration by slowing down the backswing and turning your weight into the right side. That right foot should be firmly planted and the shift of weight contained within the swing. Don't sway back, lose your center of gravity and fall off the ball. Most women don't pivot. They jerk away from the ball instead of turning. If to the best of your ability you keep your head in place and make your whole left side revolve around your right hip, you'll develop the turning action that's needed.

*Sandy shows how the hips should turn on the backswing (opposite page). With one hand on the club and other hand empty she shows move back into the ball on downswing.*

When you have reached the top of the swing—the short irons will never quite reach a full swing—a slight lateral movement toward the left begins. Here the acceleration of the clubhead starts, and as you unwind from the right side, the hips and legs turn into the downswing. For women it is the hips and legs which

116

*On the downswing Sandy moves
into her left side, shifting
hips out of the way at impact.*

*Swing continues in these pictures. Note right knee (left below) bends more; weight shift is completed (below).*

create power. To understand this left lateral movement, think of the left hip as backing into the ball. Such a movement allows the clubface to stay longer with the ball and thus increases power on the shot.

## ALIGNMENT

After acceleration, the next biggest problem is alignment. I am forever having problems with setting myself toward the flag. With these shorter irons we are naturally aiming for that flag. A good short iron can make up for a lack of distance off the tee and fairway, but the shot has to be close. Accuracy is the key.

When I get off my swing and start missing the green or leaving myself too many long putts as a result of a missed short iron, I return to the fundamentals and work on alignment. Your swing may be near-perfect, but if you are setting yourself off the flag, that's where the ball will land.

Test your alignment with two clubs. (I carry a

yardstick with me to the practice tee when I'm checking my alignment.) Set the two clubs on the ground in a T-formation. Then at the address see that all parts of your body are square to the target.

On wedge shots into the green, however, I take a narrower stance and set myself up open. But if I am hitting full seven-, eight- and nine-irons into the green, I am square.

When I position myself, my left side and shoulders are slightly higher at the address. My right elbow is tucked in close to the side. My feet are a bit farther apart than my shoulders, a little wider apart than normal. I do this because of my size and the need to turn as much weight as possible into the shot.

I start the club back by keeping it low to the ground. My wrists just begin to break when they are waist-high. I shift weight by bending or kicking in the left foot. Most of my weight has moved over to the right side, but you'll notice in the pictures that I have not pulled off the ball. My head has kept its position directly over the ball. I have not turned my hands one way or the other, but simply let them follow the natural turn of the swing on the backswing.

At the top of my swing, my left shoulder is under my chin, and my left arm is completely extended. You can also see that my right elbow has kept itself close to the body. It doesn't point off down the fairway. As I begin the downswing, my weight shifts back to the left side, and the left side begins to firm itself up for the moment of impact. Notice in the action photos the position of the left knee. As I begin to drive down on the ball, my left hip turns out of the way to give me room to move. My left arm is still extended and guiding the club down and back to the ball. I have kept the balance of my body behind the shot. Observe the location of my head. This ensures that my power—particularly in the legs and hips—is driving at the ball. It is in the hips and legs that women have their greatest strength, and they must develop this strength in the golf swing. At the moment of impact, all my weight is

*On the backswing Sandy kicks
in her left knee, but she does
not pull off the ball. The
majority of her weight has
moved to the right side. On
the downswing she shifts back
to the left side.*

on the left side. Notice the way my left foot is turned on edge and the relaxed attitude of my right leg.

Once I have hit the ball, my hands follow the flight, turning over as the centrifugal force completes the swing. My whole body has turned toward the hole to watch the flight of the shot. I have finished high, and the force of the follow-through carries me around to the full completion of the arc.

## THE SOFT IRON

Often you will want to hit a soft iron into the green—a nine-iron that you will want to hold on the green

*The correct grip has all the fingers close together in an overlapping grip (opposite page). Grip is kept firm throughout the swing (right).*

without any roll. This is not a difficult shot to play, if you will make a few alterations on your basic short-iron swing.

Begin by shortening your grip on the club; take off two or three inches. This will station you closer and lower to the ball. Next, open the face of the club dramatically, but don't change your grip. On this shot be sure that your hands are still ahead of the ball. Your weight will be mainly on the left side, and you won't have much of a pivot.

This shot depends on the flow of the clubhead through the ball. There is very little strength involved. What is important is the breaking of the wrists. You do this quickly as you start the club back. Let the right hand take over the flip through the shot. The ball will pop up from the lie and carry high into the green. It is the combination of height and the cutting action of the clubhead through the ball that makes the ball grab on the green.

One more thing about irons: Most women use irons that are too heavy for them or irons with shafts that are too stiff. They just aren't able to swing these clubs properly. I would advise any woman to consult a professional before buying a set of clubs, or at least to play a round of golf with the set first. The right club in your hands can make the game of golf much easier. Don't put yourself at a disadvantage from the very beginning. We all need as much help as we can get if we're going to play respectable golf.

*Sandy takes back the iron with right elbow tucked close to the body (opposite page).*

# POINTS TO REMEMBER

1. Hit the short irons from a square stance with the ball positioned slightly ahead of center.

2. Keep the left arm fully extended to ensure a full arc on the swing.

3. Check your alignment often with these short clubs by placing the clubs down along the intended line of flight.

4. Accelerate throughout the downswing to gain clubhead speed at impact and maximum power on the shot.

5. Take a full pivot and turn of the shoulders. The whole left side moves away from the ball with the hands and clubhead.

6. Keep your weight evenly balanced between both feet except on the soft nine-iron shots. The weight then is on the left foot.

7. Make sure your irons aren't too heavy or your shafts too stiff.

*These three pictures show the good hip turn Sandy possesses. A good turn helps generate power in the swing.*

# Mary Mills

# Playing the Wedge from Grass and Sand

Mary Mills is an outstanding short-game player with a superb swing. Born in 1940 in Laurel, Mississippi, she has been playing golf since the age of 11. After graduating from Millsaps College with a degree in philosophy, she turned professional and was named Rookie of the Year in 1962. She has been among the top 20 money-winners every year. Among her six LPGA victories are the 1963 USGA Women's Open and the 1964 LPGA Championship. Her last tour victory was the 1970 Immke Buick Open in Columbus, Ohio. In 10 years on the tour Mary has won over $136,000 in prize money. In November, 1972, Mary and five other tournament professionals toured South Africa in a special golf exhibition series.

**Grip:** The wedge is choked an inch or two down the shaft. This creates better control of the heavier clubhead and permits the body to get closer to the ball. Hands are firm, but not frozen on the shaft.

**Stance:** Feet are as wide apart as the shoulders, with the left foot slightly back to create an open position toward the line of flight. Ball is played off the left instep on most wedge shots. Knees are flexed and arms are comfortable.

**Swing:** A one-piece motion with no single part—hands, arms or knees—dominating the swing. Length of the backswing is gauged by the distance from the flag or the lie. Wrists are cocked sooner than on a normal swing, and the wedge face, which is open at address, is kept open throughout the swing. The wedge is taken back along the line so as to create a cutting action that establishes backspin on the shot.

**Club Selection:** Women should always carry a sand or pitching wedge, preferably both. They produce different types of shots. If only one is carried, it should be the sand wedge. It's more versatile.

**Major Problem:** Generating enough clubhead speed so that the wedge does not "die" at the point of impact. Women tend to be afraid to hit through this shot in the sand or to strike the pitching wedge boldly when in grass close to the green. These shots do not require strength, but they do need an authoritative swing.

## THE LONG WEDGE

*How much of a swing does it take to hit a wedge thirty or forty yards? How do I find the proper direction? Where should the ball land on the green? How do I create backspin?*

These are the types of questions I am frequently

*The wedge is an important club when you're close to the green and need loft and backspin (opposite page).*

*Keep down on the wedge shot
even after the ball is hit.*

*Make sure you follow through*
*on the shot and complete the*
*swing as you would on an iron.*

asked about the pitching wedge. The wedge to most women seems like a new club, an "extra" club, because it isn't one of the basic golfing irons. Most women aren't sure when to play the wedge, or whether to play it at all.

I think the wedge is essential! It revolutionized the game of golf when it was first introduced. I don't know how I would score if I couldn't use the wedge. It's a stroke saver on almost every hole. And it is an easy club to hit, once you gain the feel for it.

The way to learn to use the wedge is to take a few lessons from your local professional and then go onto a practice area and work with it. You have to learn how hard to hit with the club and what distances you'll cover with your swing. You have to learn how the ball will react on the green and what sort of bounce and roll you'll get. Playing the wedge, you'll get a higher loft and a softer shot, and the ball will be "played with" by the wind. Therefore, you have to know what to do in certain situations. Unless these factors are taken into consideration, a good chip with a wedge can turn into an unsuccessful shot.

First of all, with the wedge you must have the proper line and the correct address at the ball.

I get the proper address by placing my right foot into position, then bringing my left foot onto the line of flight. Once I know where I'm aiming, I drop back the left foot one or two inches. I am now in an open stance. Most—if not all—wedge shots are hit from this stance.

With my open stance I will naturally cut across the ball with a normal swing, and this cutting action will create backspin. With backspin I am more likely to hold the ball on the green and get the ball close to the hole.

Before you do anything else with the wedge, make sure you are getting the correct line. If you find you're striking all your pitch shots in a pattern to the right or left of the pin, study your address. Make an adjustment in the stance and hit again. Keep adjusting until the

*The left foot is drawn back off the line of flight (opposite page).*

*Use the Sandy Palmer method to check stance and direction.*

ball is flying toward the pin. Don't compensate by swinging at the ball in a different way. Have someone check your direction, or put a club down yourself along the line of your feet (before dropping back the left foot) and see where you have yourself pointed. Sandy Palmer carries a yardstick in her bag for just that reason. When she's on the practice tee, you can see her checking direction with that yardstick.

Grip all wedge shots down an inch or two on the shaft; for very short chip shots, grip down more. There are several reasons for this. You don't need a big swing. The arc will be three-quarters at the very most, and you don't require the full length of the club. The stance is not wide; it is only the width of your shoulders. You're not going to make a big turn of the hips. And with less club to work with, you have better control and better feel for the shot.

The ball is played anywhere between the left instep and the middle of the stance, depending on your feel. If you want to loft the shot particularly high, play the ball off the left toe and hit the shot on the upswing.

The face of the wedge is also played open. This is done by taking a normal grip on the shaft and then turning the left hand slightly, so that an additional knuckle shows on the grip. By having an open face, you are able to achieve more loft and obtain more backspin.

It is necessary to feel comfortable with the pitching wedge, so move about until you are at ease. Most women make two mistakes here: They don't flex their knees, and they reach for the ball. Therefore, they never quite feel at home on the wedge.

At the address bend your knees a fraction just to get the tension out of them. Make sure, however, that you have the whole weight of your body evenly distributed from toe to heel upon your feet, and between both feet. Next, make sure you aren't reaching for the shot. Let your arms hang naturally with the club in your hand. The ball should be within easy reach. The pitching wedge shot is a snug shot.

Depending on how I'm feeling, I think first about

*The hands should be placed several inches down the shaft for better swing control. Play the ball back in the stance (opposite page) and open the face of the wedge.*

either swinging through the shot or setting up rhythm in my legs or pulling with my left arm. It depends on my mood. Often one of those "feelings" comes up, seems right and helps me hold the shot together. You'll get similar sensations in your game, and it's wise to capitalize on those moods. But nevertheless, it's the whole swing, not a combination of "feelings," that makes the shot.

Many professionals think one or the other hand controls the shot. Tommy Armour says to hit the ball with the right hand, while Bob Toski likes to let the left side dominate on the wedge. I personally try to hit the ball with both hands, using them as a unit. I also move my body and my hands in one piece. I don't think that either the body or the hands should lead the shot. A smooth swing means working with the hands.

The major problem women have with the wedge is getting speed on the swing. Power is generated only by swinging with authority. My swing is not any easy "ladylike" approach. I *swing* that club! I do this by gradually accelerating the clubhead through the backswing and into the shot. Don't worry about hitting the wedge too far. You get much more loft with this club, especially with the open face, and you can control the distance by regulating the length of the backswing. If you hit the wedge and vary the length of your backswing, you'll soon gauge the length needed for different shots.

Distance is determined by the power generated in the downswing, not by forcing the follow-through on the wedge. The follow-through on any shot should be a natural result of the clubhead speed moving through the ball. Let the follow-through act on its own, and don't force the finish.

The wedge shot is the same as any other shot off the fairway, with one difference. On all wedge shots you cock the wrists sooner than normal. It is not a sud-

*Get close to the ball at the address by bending knees and gripping club down the shaft (opposite page).*

143

den cock—as in the sandtraps—but it is a quicker break than you use with the other irons. Once again, this quick cocking of the wrists will aid in the development of backspin.

Getting the ball to stop close to the flag is what the wedge is all about. Women aren't conscious enough of that fact. They don't take into consideration the slope of the green, the wind or the placement of the pin. They are too easily satisfied with just getting on the green. Well, that's not enough. Getting close to the flag is what the game is all about.

First of all, know where the pin is. But more importantly, know where you want the ball to land on that particular green. Gauge how much roll you think you'll get on the green. If you're hitting into a surface that slopes away from you, it will be very hard to hold the ball. Therefore, pitch way short of the flag. When the weather is dry and the greens aren't watered, the ball will shoot across short grass; again you'll have to play cautiously. Knowing what type of surface you're chipping toward will aid your shot. Since there's lots of room for error with the wedge, a little extra thought can make even those "near misses" work for you.

## THE SOFT WEDGE

A slight variation on the wedge shot helpful to most women is a shot we professionals call the soft wedge. It is used when the ball has to land softly on the green or when there is little green to work with. It is also used over a bunker and where the pin is tucked up close to the edge of the green. It is a shot that can save strokes.

I take the same setup I have in the sand. That is, I play the ball off the left foot or left instep. I have an open stance to the line and take the club back directly along that line. But the major difference of the soft wedge from the normal one is that I swing the former with a "dead swing."

Actually, I am not swinging the club so much as I am carrying it back and coming into the ball with little increase in acceleration. There is constant but slow speed throughout the swing. The most important thing to remember is setting up that tempo of the swing. I do this by concentrating on my knee action. I get my knees moving on the shot. I don't worry about keeping my head down or getting the ball high enough. These aspects will take care of themselves if I have the club moving with a slow, steady speed.

Getting comfortable over the shot is most important. The shot depends on your ability to be relaxed. It is, therefore, a hard shot to play when you're tense about your game. It will help tremendously if you will remember not to use your wrists and to keep the club relaxed in your hands. Your arms should literally feel dead on this shot.

Take the club back again with the clubface open, but this time don't allow the face to turn over naturally on the follow-through. Keep the clubface in an open position to the flag throughout the shot. At the most you'll have a short, half-backswing and little follow-through.

The feet are as wide apart as the shoulders, and there is little turning of the hips. This shot is taken with relaxed arms. This soft wedge is almost a shot where the player is out of the action. The club does it all. It is a useful and important shot to know.

From such a shot the ball will pop up high into the air and float toward the green. Because of the stance and the open clubface, the ball will hold quickly on the putting surface. This extra shot is handy to have in your repertory, but I would advise you first to learn the normal wedge before attempting the soft wedge. If you are serious about the game, you should learn how to play both shots well. They can keep you out of trouble and get you close enough to the pin to score.

One area where I consider women weak in their golf game is the variety of shots they know. Too often

*On the follow-through, stay down on the shot all the way. Notice the head position.*

*Playing the soft wedge, keep
the blade open and knees bent.
Notice (above, and opposite page)
the big movement of the knees.*

they are able to hit only one kind of wedge or one type of chip. By learning the soft wedge, they will have at least some option when they're around the green. And women are particularly good at those shots which require grace and finesse. Knowing how to use the wedge can make up for their lack of distance off the tee and fairway.

## THE SAND WEDGE

Why are many women leery of the sand wedge? Perhaps it is because the wedge is such an ungainly-looking club. It's heavy and awkward to grip, especially with that extra weight on the flange. There are also many unknowns with sand: the quality of the sand itself, the proper address and the length of the swing. But if a woman considers each problem separately, she's less likely to become rattled. There are several types of sand shots; I'd like to discuss each of them individually.

## DRY SAND

If the lie is normal, the ball sitting up in dry sand, there is little initial problem with the shot. I set myself up with an open stance to the line of flight by dropping back my left foot an inch or two. The width of my stance is the same as the width of my shoulders. I play the ball slightly forward of my left instep, and I make sure I'm not reaching for the ball. As with almost all shots from the sand, the blade of the wedge is open.

I work my feet down into the sand. This ensures a solid stance, since there is very little turning action on the shot. Because the feet are buried in the sand, the body is naturally lower to the ball. Therefore, I grip down an inch on the shaft of the club. This compensates for the lower position.

In the normal swing you take the club back along the line, cocking the wrists very early. This gives the

*A complete swing is made but with little acceleration (opposite page).*

151

shot a slight cutting action, which helps get the ball through the sand and also produces that backspin on the green. This cutting action is not so severe as that produced by taking the club abruptly outside the line and cutting across the ball dramatically. Therefore, there's less chance of an error on this shot. Though there is still a cutting action, it is simply the result of the open stance and the open face of the sand wedge.

Once I'm set up correctly, I must determine how hard to hit the sand shot. There are two methods of getting distance in a trap. One is to take different amounts of sand with the same swing. The other is to vary the length of the swing. Depending on where I am in the trap, the type of lie and the texture of the sand, I will use one method or the other.

Usually, however, instead of worrying about whether to take an inch or two behind the ball, I work on the length of the swing and the speed of the clubhead. But I do think that the average golfer should pick out a spot behind the ball and hit for that spot. This will assure her of not hitting the ball clean. You must get used to hitting through sand. It has a "feel" entirely different from playing a similar shot from the fairway.

I use the technique of drawing in the sand two parallel lines between which the ball would be positioned and trying to swing through those lines. I try to take a smooth divot of about 12 inches long. If you do this 20 times whenever you practice, you'll get over the fear of taking sand in the trap. Women—and men, too—tend to think the club won't go through the sand, but it will. The only real ways to get over reservations about the sand trap is to practice and to get help from your local professional.

The biggest mistake women make in the sand is not generating enough speed on the swing, so that they leave the club in the sand at that point of impact. They also set up with a square stance at the ball and have their wedge square at the address, keeping the clubhead from getting through the sand.

*Concentrate more on arm
motion than pivot in the swing.*

*Normal swing is taken but
little pivot required.*

*A half swing at most is needed. The left arm should pull club back to the ball.*

*Body is positioned open to the line of flight. Mary indicates line of flight and stance.*

156

When I begin my downswing, my weight is moving toward the left side. At impact, all my weight has transferred to that left side. This way I avoid "skinning" the shot. When the weight isn't on the left side, the clubhead can bounce up into the ball. Taking the club back immediately breaks the wrists. This creates a very upright swing, a "sharp-looking" swing. I never take more than a three-quarter swing on these sand-shots.

Beginning the downswing, I throw the right hand into the action. This helps generate that power needed to get through the shot. Knowing that I'm already aiming three or four inches behind the ball, I'm not worried about cutting the shot short and hitting the ball directly. When working on this shot, try to think of

*In sand, work both feet down to achieve solid stance.*

slicing a thin layer of sand with the wedge. If you can picture this, you should be okay.

If you have a long wedge from the sand—that is, the green is still a good distance from you—make a few simple changes in your swing. I keep the clubhead square and play the ball back toward the middle of my stance. I don't grip down on the club, but I do plan on taking at least an inch of sand. I also take a longer and bigger swing at the ball.

## BURIED SHOTS

Most people think that the buried shot, sometimes called the "fried egg," is hard to hit, but actually it isn't. The setup—either with an open or square stance—depends on how far you have to hit the ball. The big problem on this shot is that the ball will roll a lot.

What I want to do is get the ball out of the trap. If I leave the clubface open, the club won't get through the sand, so I have to make the shot with a square or even hooded blade. By closing the blade I increase the roll. There is really no way to cut this ball out of the sand.

If I have a short distance to go, I will play the ball off my left foot. This means that I will catch the ball more on the upswing. Because the clubhead has struck the sand first, the impact will be less severe. If I want to send the ball a long way, I will play it back toward center. Then I won't dig quite as much behind the ball, and there will be less sand between the clubface and the ball. I can get distance this way.

On both of these shots my swing is very abrupt. I take the club back almost in the shape of a V. That is, I start out with a quick breaking of the wrists and then throw the clubhead down into the sand. I don't even worry about my follow-through on these shots. The other point to remember is: Don't lose control of the clubhead. There is a tendency to let loose of the club when it is thrown back into the sand. Make sure you have finished the swing.

*Keep the blade of the wedge open. This ensures getting through the sand shot (opposite page).*

159

## WET SAND

For playing the ball off wet sand, I advise you to change clubs and use a pitching wedge. It is a lighter club, and there is less likelihood of the club flange bouncing off the hard surface. On this swing be careful to cut the ball and catch it thin. There will be less sand—and what there is will be wet—between the clubface and the ball.

It is important to be open on this swing, both in the stance and the clubface. Your body should be turned about a 45-degree turn away from the line and the clubface turned open. This is a very soft shot, with no strength needed—just a smooth swing that slows through the ball toward the target. Claude Harmon suggests that to make sure you're "open" with the blade, you should check the position of your clubface on the follow-through. If the face of the clubhead is pointed up and the club is extended toward the target, you're in good shape.

In the wet-sand shot it is especially important to break the wrists early on the backswing and not to hurry the shot. This is perhaps the "softest" shot to be made from the bunker because the ball will bounce high and run. If you remember to keep everything open, you will generate backspin and keep the ball under control.

## FALLAWAY BUNKER SHOT

At times in a round of golf, you will find yourself caught in a sand trap up close to the front slope: an almost impossible place to play from. On this shot you are under the lip and mainly concerned with balance. You don't have to worry about hitting behind the ball, because you are already set to do that by the unnatural position of your stance. Your biggest problem is balance. But instead of fighting it, just hit into the ball and let yourself fall down the hill after you have made the shot.

The secret of success on this one is making sure that the tilt of your body parallels the position of the ball. Your shoulder-line should parallel the rise in the hill. Let your weight settle naturally on your right foot and swing up on the shot. The ball will fly out high, but it can be controlled if your clubface is open at contact. Usually you'll be playing this shot from a posi-

*A buried shot or "fried egg"*
*looks like this, but ball can*
*be played out safely.*

On buried shots, close the
face of the club and play the
ball more off the left foot.
Hit through the ball.

Keep everything open on wet
sand (opposite page). This may be
the easiest trap shot to hit.

162

tion very close to the green, so you won't have much distance to worry about. To keep yourself close to the ball, make sure you grip down a few inches on the shot.

## DOWNHILL BUNKER SHOT

Play the downhill bunker shot almost the same as the fall-away bunker shot. Your shoulders are tilted to agree with the slope. Your weight, let's say, is now entirely on the left side. Also, you must open the clubface a lot; because the club will be driving down to the ball at a sharper angle, you need to build in all the loft you can. Your open stance should be accentuated to balance the extreme open position of the clubface.

Remember to hit this shot. Most women have a tendency to lift or try to scoop the ball from the sand. It never works. On any successful shot from the trap, the secret is a controlled, smooth swing that makes contact with the sand, goes under and through the ball and finishes. Swing that way and you won't have trouble with sand.

*On the fallaway bunker shot, balance is the biggest factor. Set yourself according to the slope of the lie.*

*Mary Mills (opposite page)*
*swings through the shot. Don't*
*bury club in sand. Judy Rankin*
*keeps left arm stiff in*
*making the same type of shot.*

# POINTS TO REMEMBER

1. Grip a few inches down on the shaft for better control of the wedge.

2. Distance is not as important as alignment. Continually check your direction, especially with the fairway wedge.

3. With the wedge always use an open stance and, on most shots, an open position of the blade.

4. Play the ball forward in the stance on all shots.

5. On the wedge cock the wrists early in the backswing.

6. Generate power on the shot through the downswing.

7. Take some sand on all trap shots. The darker the sand, the less you'll need to take.

*Making the shot to the green with the wedge (three-picture sequence) means a steady position over the ball and a free, steady arm movement.*

# Pam Barnett

# Putting
# on and off
# the Green

Pam Barnett, from Charlotte, North Carolina, turned professional in 1966 after graduating from Winthrop College in Rock Hill, South Carolina. Pam, who was born in 1944, began to play golf at the age of six. She won the Southgate Ladies Open in 1971 and earned $18,000 that year on the tour. In her short professional career she has won over $67,000. One of the many attractive new women on the tour as well as one of the finest putters among the professionals, she offers some sound advice in this chapter on the most important stroke of the game.

**Grip:** The reverse overlap grip is used on the green. Reverse the little finger of the right hand and the left-hand index finger. Or use the ten-finger grip with all fingers on the shaft of the club. The hands should fit together on the club with the back of the left hand and the palm of the right hand both facing the target.

**Stance:** It is important to be comfortable over the ball, with a stance square to the line of putt. The eyes must be directly over the ball to achieve the correct perspective for direction. Stance can be either wide or narrow. Comfort is the only consideration.

**Swing:** The blade and butt end of the putter move as one piece. The putter blade accelerates through the stroke to keep the putt on line. Putter should be taken back as far as it will go forward.

**Club Selection:** Select a putter that feels comfortable in the hand. Don't change putters needlessly. If putting goes sour, stay with your blade. It's usually your stroke at fault, not your putter.

**Major Problem:** Keeping loose, comfortable and steady over the putt. If you are not relaxed on the putt, the stroke becomes tense and jerky. The most important aspect of putting is the ability to be at ease when you are over the ball.

Putting is one place on the golf course where women are definitely equal to men. There is no need for strength in putting, and good "touch" with the putter is not peculiar to either sex. If most women have trouble on the green, it's because they don't concentrate enough. They are satisfied with getting down in two putts, when they should be trying for the one-putt instead. To be a good putter, you must block out all distractions on the green and pay strict attention to the job at hand.

One way to develop concentration is to think

about making the putt immediately on reaching the green. Study the roll of the surface and speed of the grain, and then decide on the line and make the putt. To help your concentration, don't take too much time. Try to make quick decisions, and, once over the ball, putt immediately. This way, you avoid lingering doubts about how to stroke the ball. Usually the first decision on line is the most accurate. Don't second-guess yourself out of a putt.

To be a reasonably good putter, you must believe you are going to make the putt every time. This is especially true of five- and six-foot putts. If you are only attempting to get close to the hole on these lengths, you have little chance to become a good putter. There is no reason to think you can't make them. Strive to reduce your putting total by at least ten putts a round. Get into the habit of keeping two scores: one for your total game and one just for putting. If you can reduce your putting total, your score for the 18-hole round will drop too.

Putting, like personality, is very individual. But there are a few fundamentals that apply to everyone's stroke and need to be studied.

## GRIP

In putting both hands and all your fingers are involved. The grip normally used is the reverse overlap. Some players use the 10-finger grip. The grip should be set so that the back of the left hand and the palm of the right are both facing the target. By arranging the hands this way, there is less likelihood of turning the club over or under the stroke and throwing the ball off-line.

I try to obtain a square stance, square to the line toward the hole. I make sure that I'm in a comfortable position and bending from the waist. My knees are also bent. In putting you must keep the tension out of your arms, because tension causes you to jerk the blade. You want the blade to have freedom, a small swinging

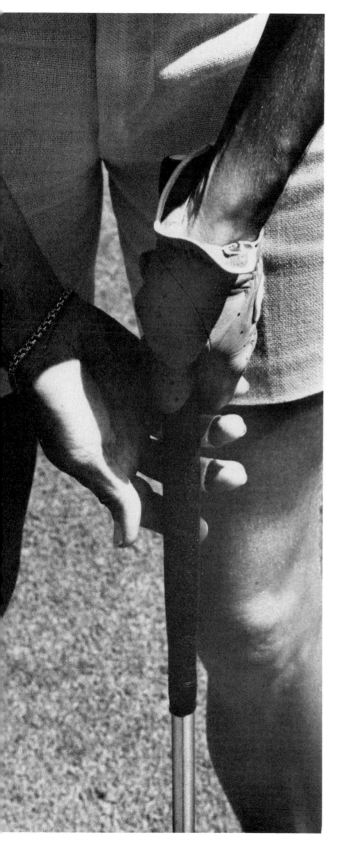

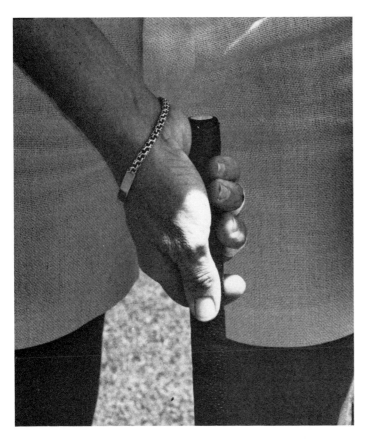

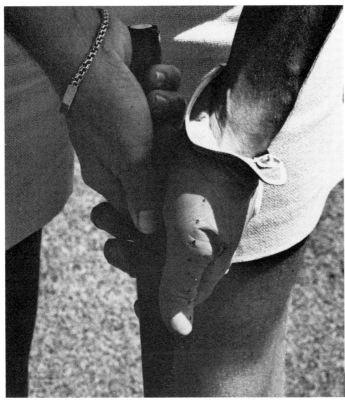

*The normal putting grip is the left hand on top (opposite page). Pam Barnett putts cross-handed as shown here.*

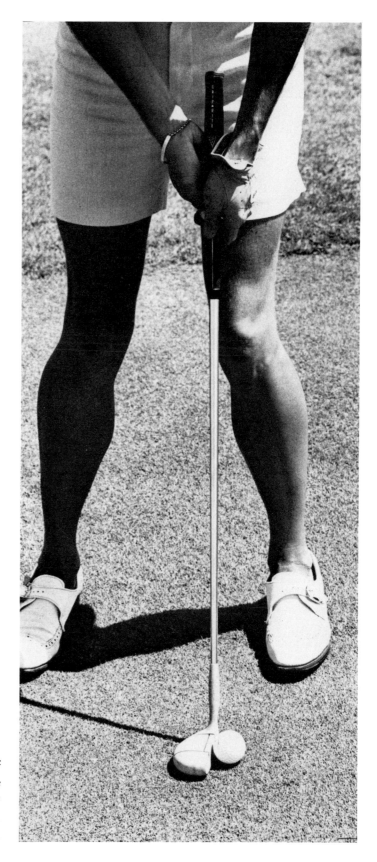

*Pam positions the ball off
her left foot. Her grip is
down the shaft of
the club (opposite page).
This gives better control.*

effect. I try to keep my hands loose on the grip, so as to get "feel" into the fingers. Also—and this is most important—I move the butt end of the putter and the blade back and forth together. To eliminate error, I use little or no wrist action in my putting stroke.

## LINE

I pick a line along which I want the ball to travel to the hole. I then stroke the ball along that line. I don't worry much about the speed of the putt, because my attention is directed toward rolling the ball along that line. That is one way to simplify putting.

To get the correct line, I look at the putt from at least two angles: from behind the ball and from the other side of the cup. I always pick a line that moves directly toward the hole so that I am putting on a straight line. That's a lot easier than a curving or a spot putt. On spot putting you pick a spot you want the ball to pass over, but usually when you hit for it, the ball dies before it reaches the hole. I for one never seem to be able to hit the ball hard enough under those circumstances.

Regardless of the speed of a green, always remember to accelerate into the putt. If the greens are particularly fast, then you must control the backswing. You can tell the speed of the green several ways. If the grass—as you look straight down at it—appears shiny or glassy, then you have a fast surface. If the grass is a darker green, it means that the grain is growing against you and that the ball won't roll as fast. Very often the grass will appear shiny in one patch and darker in another, so you won't know which way the grain is growing. Check the grass in a three-foot radius around the hole. Use that section to make your decision about speed. Since most women play one course very often, they are soon familiar with the kinds of greens on it, and the problem of speed becomes less difficult.

It does seem at times that we study the putt too

long and from too many angles. We tend in those situations to see too much. Such readings of the green don't help, but serve more to confuse. When you think that has happened to you, concentrate on looking at the line from behind the ball to the cup and go ahead and putt.

Some of the best putters I know are women who only play once or twice a week. The reason for this, I think, is that they don't worry much about line, break or speed. They just get out there and putt. I've noticed this in the Pro-Am events we play. The local gals often out-putt the professionals.

## SHORT PUTTS

On these "knee knockers" of two feet or so, it is important that you remain steady over the ball. Try to keep a comfortably loose grip on the club. You are putting for a short distance, so the backstroke will be a matter of inches. Concentrate on that relatively short stroke. Get it under control and keep the blade straight and moving toward the hole. You still have to accelerate through the ball, even for a short distance. If you don't, you're likely to be jabbing at the ball.

Normally on such short putts you won't have to worry about extreme breaks. The ball won't have a chance to fall off rapidly unless you are coming dramatically downhill at the hole. Try to putt the ball for a part of the hole. Don't be afraid. If a putt is struck firmly, a break in the grain won't affect the roll. Even on these short putts I line up from behind the ball, picking a line from the ball to the cup. I think about rolling the ball along that line instead of trying to make the putt. It seems to take the pressure off.

## MEDIUM PUTTS

On these putts I am especially careful about picking the right line to the hole. I look at the putt from both angles, back and front, and maybe even from the side.

*Pam takes two putters with her on the tour. She feels the freedom to choose gives her psychological lift if her game goes sour. The two types of putters she uses are the bull's-eye (opposite page) and the mallet-head (left).*

I pick a straight line to the hole, not a curving one. I don't change my stance or the position of my legs, but if I have to go over rough grass, I play the ball off my left toe and pick up more overspin on the putt.

It is necessary to be steady on these putts. You can move off a putt just as you can move off your swing. It always helps to relax and to remember to keep your head steady even after you have stroked the ball. Again, you have to be over the ball on these putts. To check that you are, a simple method is to take your position with the blade behind the ball, then pick up the club and see that the butt end of the putter comes directly to your eyes.

Women should not blame their putter when things start going wrong on the green. I have two types of

181

*Make sure your eyes are over
the ball. Test head position with
this method of Pam's.*

putters, a bulls-eye and a mallet head, and I will switch from time to time just to give myself a little different feel on the green. But I stay with my two putters. If you get into a bad putting slump, usually your stroke is causing the trouble. But sometimes the problem can be faulty alignment, or you might be easing into the putt instead of stroking the ball, or you might not have your eye over the ball. Check to see whether you are committing these basic errors. Don't rush off to buy another putter.

## LONG PUTTS

When you have a really long putt with lots of roll between the ball and the hole, try to get close to the cup. You can't expect to drop the putt, so pretend that there is a wider circle—perhaps three feet—around the flag, and putt for that circle. Hitting the ball into that circle won't be as difficult as putting for the cup.

Look to see generally what the line will be on the

*When putting from off the left foot, stance is still square and thumb of the left hand is straight down shaft.*

putt, then mark the line you want. On these putts be careful not to lose acceleration because of the distance involved. Also, be careful not to steer the putt. If you are conscious of moving both ends of the putter at the same time, you won't have to worry about steering.

Think of the putter as one piece from the head all the way to the shoulder, and try to keep everything moving together. On these long putts especially, make sure you take the club back smooth and low to the ground. Too often players tend to lift the club on the backswing because they think they have to bang the ball toward the cup. It's not necessary. If it is a particularly long putt—60 feet or more and uphill—just lengthen the backstroke and steadily accelerate into the ball; you'll get the putt close to the flag.

## OTHER PUTTING METHODS

One other putting method that works for many women is spreading the hands on the shaft of the club. This is

*This series of pictures shows Pam making a long putt. She stays down even after striking the ball. She judges speed and distance of the putt by eye (opposite page).*

useful for women who putt with their shoulders. That is, the shoulder turn is their only motion when they stroke the putt. This keeps them from turning the blade of the putter with an independent arm motion. When the hands are spread down the shaft on the putt, they cover a larger space, and wrist action is eliminated. It is actually the shoulders that make the putt.

I putt cross-handed on the tour. That is, my right hand is on top of the shaft, my left hand below it. The reason I do this is that my stroke was too big on the backswing. I found myself easing into the ball at impact. In other words, I would de-accelerate on the stroke and had no real control. So I tried putting cross-handed to keep my backstroke in control. I think it's a good method, especially for short putts, when you need control over the blade. It also tends to make both hands work together as a unit instead of getting wristy. This cross-handed method also keeps the hands out of the putt. It allows the butt end of the putter and the blade to operate square to the target.

You can't really copy someone else's putting. You

*On the putting stroke keep
the blade low to the ground.
Don't pick up the blade.*

*On long putts lengthen the backstroke but do not slam the ball. Keep the stroke long, low and smooth. Note how putter follows through.*

must develop your own style and stroke. Nevertheless, all professional golfers agree that it is important to be relaxed over the ball and to get a comfortable grip and stance. As long as you keep both ends of the club moving together, you can do almost anything you want and still be a good putter.

*Cross-handed putting helps Pam control backstroke.*

I try to putt the same way I swing the club. The backswing is just the setting motion for the putt. I start accelerating from the point where the backswing is completed and then continue on through the ball. If you tend to ease into the putt, the ball won't hold the line. You'll end up directing the ball toward the hole rather than stroking it.

## PUTTING FROM OFF THE GREEN

When you are putting from off the green, from the short grass, you have to be particularly careful about the grain. If the grain is against you, strike the ball more firmly to get it moving. Also, the ball may have a tendency to bounce, especially if the grass at the edge of the green is heavy and flush. This can throw your line off. If the ground is just too matty or wet and you have several feet to cover before reaching the surface of the green, it's best to go with an iron and chip the ball clear of that frog hair.

However, if the grass is dry and trim, use the putter. I believe that for most women the putter is the better club with a frog-hair shot. Women tend not to get as much practice with the four- and five-irons, so they are not as comfortable with these clubs. The putter is better-controlled in these situations. It's easier to get the ball close to the cup when you're rolling it across a green. There are just too many chances for error in short chips. A good putt will get you close, and that's as much as you can expect.

If you have a particularly long uphill putt from the frog hair to the flag and it looks as if you'll have to bang the ball, it's unwise to use a putter. You don't want to press the putter beyond its normal use. Take the iron and chip the ball. But for a ball just off the green and within a few yards of the cup, the putter's the answer!

*When putting from off the green, play the ball more off the left foot to increase overspin. When on the green (opposite page), strike all short putts firmly and aim at the center of the cup.*

# POINTS TO REMEMBER

1. Use the reverse overlap grip with hands close together. Or use the 10-finger grip.

2. Concentrate on making all putts.

3. Look over the putts from at least two angles.

4. Keep the putter low to the ground on the backstroke.

5. Pick a straight line to the hole and putt along that line.

6. Make sure your eyes are directly over the ball and that you are comfortable with your stance.

7. Use the putter rather than a chipping iron from off the edge of the green.

*Don't steer the putt. These three pictures show the way Pam strikes through the ball. The blade is square at all positions of the putt.*

# Jane Blalock

# Playing the Trouble Shots with Control

This 5-foot 6-inch blue-eyed blonde from Portland, New Hampshire, has been playing golf since she was 13. She turned professional in 1969 after graduating with a degree in history from Rollins College in Florida.

"Janie" has been a leading money-winner on the tour. In 1971 she won two tournaments and over $35,000 in prize money. In 1972 she was a leading money-winner, earning over $57,000 and winning five tournament events, including first-place in the Dinah Shore Winners Circle. In 1970 and 1971 she was named Most Improved Professional.

Janie, who has been a controversial and exciting player, is considered by many to be the brightest star of the tour. In this chapter she tells how to play those difficult control shots that are needed in order to score well.

**Grip:** The grip is normal on all shots. No adjustments should be made. It is important to keep the grip consistent for all aspects of the game.

**Stance:** Feet are adjusted on the line of flight, depending on the type of shot. Ball is played between the center of the stance and on the left instep. Stance is a bit wider to maintain balance on wind shots and some uphill positions.

**Swing:** Three-quarter swing on all shots. This gives greater control and simplifies the swing.

**Club Selection:** On uphill lies always take one club more than normal, on downhill lies one club less. Play the five-wood from the fairway bunker.

**Major Problem:** Keeping the arms relaxed and free and the swing slow and steady from these different positionings. Don't press on any of the unusual lies, or the swing will tense up.

On the golf course there are shots that require great control to be executed properly. The most difficult of these is the sand shot played from the fairway bunker. The fairway wood is generally used only by good golfers in this situation.

A wood should be used from the sand trap only when there is an uphill lie and a possibility of reaching the green. If there is no possibility, I suggest taking an iron just to make sure you're out of the bunker. However, sometimes against the wind or on a par four when it's possible to get close to the target, a wood from the sand is worth the gamble.

The first thing I do when confronted with this shot is to take a five-wood to ensure that I'll get enough loft without forcing. I choke down two or three inches because, as you know, when you take a stance in the sand trap, you bury yourself a couple of inches. If you

*On wood shots from the bunker
get a solid stance in
the sand and grip down an inch
or so on the club.*

197

handle the club at the normal length, you are likely to bury the clubhead in the sand on the downswing.

Before entering the trap, I put my hands on the club in the manner with which I will address the ball, and keep them firmly there. To avoid a penalty stroke, I am careful also not to heel the club in the sand when I approach the shot.

I plant my feet deep while trying to relax my body —especially my shoulders and arms—as much as possible. I pick a spot in the middle of the ball, and I concentrate on that spot when I swing. I stand with my head very still. This is most important on the bunker shot. You must keep your head still so that the arms and shoulders can swing around a pivotal point.

I swing my arms as slowly and freely as I can. I accelerate toward the target with little body motion. I try to keep a one-piece action for as long as possible, longer on this shot than on any others. I don't break my wrists, because once the wrists have been broken and the hands are cocked, I lose my arc. Likewise, if the left foot comes off the shot, it will allow me to move off the ball. For that reason, the weight transfer is not as great as on an ordinary shot. I don't want to get off the ball. This is very much a control shot, and there is no need to swing hard. The more compact and simple the swing, the less room for error. That is why the arc is so vital. I must come down exactly at the same point as when I started. The shot is precise because of the need to catch the ball clean off the sand.

If you have a downhill or a side-hill lie, I recommend you take a four- or five-iron and just get the ball back in the fairway. I use a wood out of a fairway bunker perhaps once or twice a tournament. Therefore, it's not a shot I get to practice a lot. And that makes it difficult to play. The main point to remember on this shot is to be slow, smooth and steady.

*With woods from the sand there is little body motion and the wrists are broken late (opposite page).*

## UPHILL LIE

When you are approaching an uphill lie with an iron,

*On the bunker shot pick the
ball clean off the sand.*

the address position is the most important consideration. You must put the hands ahead of the ball and
keep the left leg slightly flexed to maintain balance and
be consistent with the contour of the ground. If the
left leg is flexed and the right leg straight, it keeps your
shoulders more nearly level. Balance is especially important on these side-hill lies.

When selecting a club for an uphill lie, take one
more club than usual, and choke down on it. When
hitting uphill, you create more loft. For example, when
I'm hitting a seven-iron, the ball will react off this lie
more like an eight-iron. The trajectory off the slope is
higher than normal. Again, in any kind of trouble shot,
I advocate a three-quarter swing for better control.

Also, on the uphill lie the ball tends to hook. Depending on the length of the shot, I would aim five to
ten yards right of the target. The ball will be coming
from an inside/out pattern which will create a natural
drawing motion.

The ball is placed forward, and you must try for a
sweeping motion on the swing. The tendency is to dig
into the turf as you are coming through the shot. Let
your arms parallel the terrain on the swing-through.
Never fight the terrain; always go with it and take
advantage of the positioning.

## DOWNHILL LIE

The downhill lie is roughly the reverse of an uphill lie.
But on this shot the hands are again ahead of the ball.
The ball is played back of center so that the club will
contact it in a descending motion. In the reverse of an
uphill lie, you should take one club less. If I have an
ordinary five-iron shot, I might take a six-iron, because
the lie will take loft off the club, whereas an uphill lie
creates loft.

Since the tendency on a downhill lie is to hit the
ball from left to right, you must allow from five to ten
yards for a slight fade.

On a downhill lie the weight remains forward, and

*On uphill lies with an iron make sure hands are placed forward and the left knee is flexed. Also choke down on the club an inch or two (opposite page).*

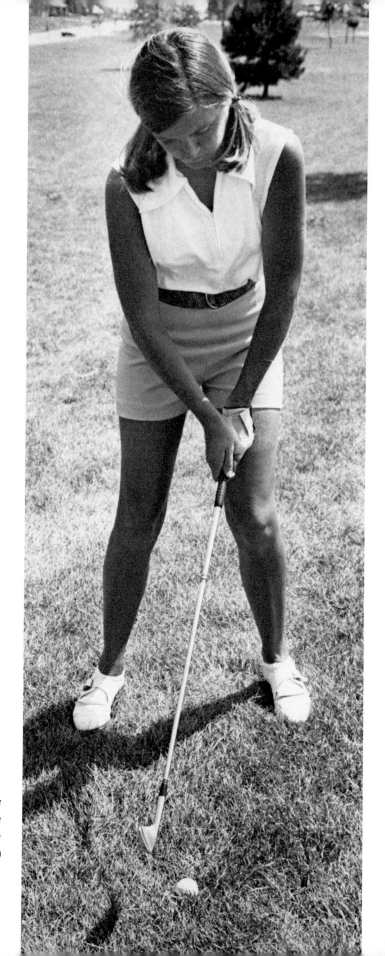

On wind shots, from either the
rough or fairway, play the
ball slightly back in the
stance and hit (opposite page)
with a three-quarter swing.

you have to swing your arms up a little more quickly. Pick the club up sooner than ordinarily on the backswing. The right leg is flexed on a downhill lie to keep the shoulders level and to maintain balance.

To achieve good balance, you may widen your stance a bit. When you swing the club back, it is easy to lose your footing and sway off the ball. On this type of lie you also tend to come up on the ball. Remember to keep your head steady all the way through the shot and to stay down even after you have made impact.

## WIND SHOTS

The shot into the wind is another control shot. Its purpose is to keep the ball low so that the wind can't affect the direction. You must take one or two more clubs than usual to make up for distance. You will be taking only a three-quarter swing, and the wind will affect the ball.

I play the ball slightly back in the stance. I make sure my hands are ahead of the ball, and I try to keep all my weight on the left side. I want to catch the ball on a descending arc to give me better control and keep the ball down, lower to the ground.

The most important point in a wind shot is the move into the ball. I try to keep both my legs flexed more than normal. You need on this swing a good strong lateral movement with the hips and knees. This helps keep your hands from turning over on the shot.

I choke down on the club, and after I complete my three-quarter swing, I drive a little more strongly and keep the blade on the ball as long as possible. In fact, I play a game with myself. I picture a dollar bill right in front of the ball, and I try to cover that dollar bill with the blade of my club, keeping it square. I keep my hands in front of the ball, and I delay my wrist break as long as I can.

## CUT SHOT

The difference between a cut shot (or slice shot) and a regular shot is the setup. On the cut shot I open my stance. I do not change my grip. Some people say to use a weak left hand for the slice, but I try to keep my grip constant on all my clubs to maintain consistency in my game.

The primary thing I work on in a cut shot is the angle in which I swing my arms to my body. I swing the cut shot outside the line going back, and I pull it inside coming through. This gives it an outside/in swing. The movement causes the cutting action. Again

*On three-quarter swings keep the blade on the ball as long as possible. Keep hands in front and delay wrist break.*

*On cut shots open the stance and the position of the hips. The grip remains the same.*

208

I try to keep my blade square after I have contacted the ball and keep my hands ahead of the clubface throughout the swing. Don't let the hands turn over. Your hands should always lead on this shot.

*On hook shots the stance is square or closed to the flag.*

## HOOK SHOT

This shot is the reverse of the cut or slice. I square my shoulders, or close them a bit. I also draw my right foot back off the line of flight. I always keep the blade square on this shot. I don't fool around with the blade of the club, opening or closing it. This is because I want consistency in my game. I will, however, swing my arms slightly inside this time and then out on the downswing, almost to the right of the target. After impact I turn the hands over and give the ball a right-to-left spin.

Between these shots—slice and hook—the major difference is in the swing, taking the club back and letting it go. For me the cut and hook shots are obtained by the manipulation of the arms. The great consideration is keeping the swing under control. Never overswing, and make sure that you are slow and steady the whole way.

*Jane maintains high plane on*
*backswing and follow-through.*

211

# POINTS TO REMEMBER

1. Never play woods from the fairway bunkers unless the lie is particularly good and the distance to be covered is worth the gamble.

2. Swing all shots with a slow, controlled swing never longer than three-quarters.

3. Keep the head steady on bunker shots, so that the body can pivot around a stationary point.

4. On uphill and downhill lies flex the knees accordingly to maintain good balance and keep the shoulders level.

5. On wind shots hit the ball on the descending arc to gain control and keep the ball low.

6. With the cut and hook shots it is the action of the arms that determines the flight of the ball. The grip should be kept the same for all shots.

7. Downhill positions require one club less to make up for lack of loft. The uphill lies require one club length more.

*On downhill lies (left) hands are played forward and ball is positioned back. Widen the stance (right) to obtain better balance. On downhill lies players tend to pull up (opposite page). Keep legs bent and stay down.*

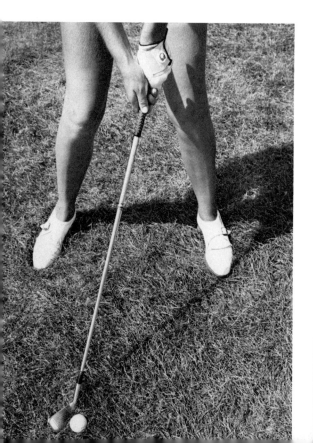

# Golf Clinic

**Do you ever feel you have all the answers to your golf game?** No, every time I tee up the ball, I learn something more about my swing and the game. Of course, the golf swing changes as we mature. That's what makes golf such a great sport. (S. H.)

**If I want to learn to play golf, how should I go about it?** Begin with lessons from a local professional. Go to a local course or driving range and have the pro teach you the proper grip and golf swing. Learn the fundamentals before playing. (K. W.)

**Should I have the same swing for all clubs?** Yes, you should. The key to golf is consistency and having a swing you can repeat. (S. H.)

**Are there different approaches to the basics of the game by the professionals?** We have all learned to play the game in certain ways, and some of us have learned bad habits we have to play with now. Yes, we vary in our techniques. One method will work for one woman, but not for another. You must experiment and find out what works for you. (S. H.)

**What is the biggest problem women golfers have?** I think it is just getting the ball off the ground. The reason this is so difficult is that women do not generate enough clubhead speed through the ball. (S. H.)

**Is there such a thing as a natural swing?** Yes there is, just as there are natural athletes. We all have natural movements that are used in the golf game. The basic swing is really very natural for most people. (S. H.)

**Are golf courses built for men? Are women at a disadvantage?** The very long courses that we play are certainly built for men. Even from the front tees they are just too long for women. We can't drive as far as men professionals. (P. B.)

**How do you develop timing?** By practice, plenty of practice. And yet sometimes I go out on the course and have no timing at all. Timing comes and goes for most people. (S. H.)

**How far should I take the club back on the driver?** The parallel position at the top of the swing is far enough. You tend to lose your grip if you go back any farther than that. (K. W.)

**I have trouble with the long irons. What should I do?** I suggest you get hold of a five- or a six-wood. They are easier clubs to hit, and they get the job done. (J. R.)

**Should I have one stance for all shots?** No, the stance varies with the type of shot you want to play. However, regardless of the stance, you must feel comfortable over the ball or you'll have trouble executing the shot. (K. W.)

**How much time should I spend practicing?** I think everyone should practice a little before playing, just to loosen up and find out how they're swinging the club. I also think women should practice on days they aren't playing, but not more than thirty minutes unless they are serious about the game and want to play professionally. (S. H.)

**How can I gain control over a particular shot?** By only swinging at the ball with a three-quarter back-swing. (S. P.)

**How fast should I swing the club?** The club speed builds up gradually through the swing and reaches its maximum at impact. But never rush the shot. You should know at all times exactly where the clubhead is. (K. W.)

**How do I keep from topping the ball?** Make sure your knees are flexed. (S. P.)

**What creates power in the swing?** A hip and shoulder turn and an extended arc. The longer the arc, the more power. (K. W.)

**How can an average golfer improve her game?** Lots of practice and lessons. I still take lessons, and every day I am learning more about the game. (S. P.)

**What do you think of the square-to-square approach to golf?** Not much. Not for women. The square-to-square method depends on strong arms and wrists. It is difficult to learn once you have learned another type of swing. I know that Sandy Haynie swings with many of the square-to-square movements, but she learned that quite early in her game. Sandy is also a very strong golfer. Square-to-square is too much for the average woman. (S. P.)

**Do you think women are naturally better around the green than men?** I don't think the professional women are better in any facet of the game. If there is one area where we might be as good, it's in chipping. That's because we do a lot of it. But the men professionals are tremendous. They can do everything! (S. P.)

**How long is the LPGA Tour?** We start in January and go until November. The tour is worth more than a million dollars in prize money now, and that means a lot more tournaments. We usually play three rounds a tournament, plus a Pro-Am. (B. B.)

**Do you think women will ever be able to compete in the same tournaments with men?** No. (P. B.)

**When should you start playing golf?** As early as possible. We have women on the tour who began to play when they were seven or eight. ( B. B. )

**Why do I have to use an overlapping grip?** The overlapping grip keeps all the fingers and both hands close together and working together on the shaft. ( K. W. )

**How far should I stand from the ball?** Just let your arms hang naturally and then take hold of the club. You'll be the right distance from the ball. ( J. R. )

**How do you handle the pressure of tournament play?** By concentration on the game. I find I get above the pressure when I play. I hear the gallery and respond to it, but people don't bother me. When I reach that point of my concentration, I am not even nervous. ( P. B. )

**Are galleries a problem for you?** No, they are really a pleasure. They add to the game. You make a lot of friends, and the harder they pull for you, the harder you try to play. ( P. B. )

**What's the biggest problem off the course for the touring professionals?** Just keeping organized. There are so many personal things to do . . . clothes to be cleaned, hair to be done and bookwork to keep up with. If you don't handle the expense account every week, it builds up into an impossible chore. ( P. B. )

**Do you have a chance to date on the tour?** It depends on the particular girl. We can go out as much as we want. A lot of women like to go out at the start of the week, but once the tournament begins, have no social life at all. Dating for me is a way to relax during a tour. Of course, getting anything very serious started in five days is pretty hard. ( B. B. )

**Is it all golf talk among the women on the tour?** Yes,

it centers around golf. Most of the players are college graduates, but when they are out here, there is little time for serious talk beyond golf. The tournament tour is all-consuming, and if we want to do well, we have to keep ourselves up mentally all the time. We have to live golf the whole while we are out here. (M. M.)

**What does women's liberation have to do with professional golf?** I don't really think it is involved. We are women who compete professionally for money. There is no way for women to take on men in golf. We can't beat them. (J. B.)

**When you win a tournament, does that key you up for the next one?** After a victory I tend to go into a slump for one or two weeks. I'm let down mentally, I guess. (J. B.)

**What happens when you lose your feel for the golf swing?** That happens quite often. I suggest that you go back to the fundamentals and try to swing the club the way you were taught. Feel will come back. (J. B.)

**Should you worry about things like being in the right position and having your hands a certain way at the top of the swing?** Some people are very conscious of club position. I get the best results when I just let the swing happen. Stand up and get comfortable. When you're comfortable, you'll get confidence. And when you're confident, you play better. (J. B.)

**How should one stand over the ball in putting?** Putting is individualistic. Use whatever works for you. Generally that will be a comfortable stance that allows you to strike the ball with an accelerated stroke. (P. B.)

**How do I keep from steering the ball?** Think of how you drive a car. By your pressing down on the accelerator, the car moves forward. Do the same thing with putting. Just strike through the ball, with the hands going on toward the hole. (P. B.)

**How do I get backspin, especially on chip shots to the green?** By hitting down and cutting across the ball. (M. M.)

**How do you keep from topping the ball on a downhill lie?** By playing the ball back in the stance. My hands are ahead, and I swing the arms up more quickly. (J. B.)

**How far should the average woman golfer hit the seven-, eight- and nine-irons?** About 110 yards for the seven, 90 yards for the eight, 75 yards for the nine. (S. P.)

**How far should I take the long irons back at the top of the swing?** I think women should let the club drop just beyond the parallel position. (S. H.)

**If I am just off the green, what should I use?** If the grass is cut short and the distance isn't great, use the putter. Otherwise take a five, six, seven or eight and hit a pitch-and-run shot. (P. B.)

**How can I increase my putting concentration?** Golf is a social game—and should remain so—but try when you're on the green to limit your conversation and think only about the putt you want to make. Relax between putts and build up concentration at the moment of the putt. (P. B.)

**How high should I tee the ball?** For the driver, tee up the ball about an inch and a quarter. (B. B.)

**What should I do if I get into a bad lie, either in the trap or rough?** Your first objective is get the ball out of trouble. Pick the club for that purpose. Don't worry about distance. (J. B.)

**Where can I find out what weight and shaft of club is**

**for me?** See a professional. He will study your swing and, according to that and your size, pick the right length and weight clubs for you. (K. W.)

**Who are the best teaching professionals?** There are many, many good ones. Bob Toski, Johnny Revolta, Harvey Penick and George Alexander are four. They have spent most of their lives teaching other pros to play golf. (S. P.)

**Besides the fundamentals, what else should you take into consideration when you are about to hit a shot?** Have an idea of where you want the ball to land, especially if you are shooting into a green. Very seldom do we actually aim at the flag. We pick out a spot on the green where we want the ball to land. Get a mental picture of the way the ball will travel before you hit the shot. (M. M.)

**Do I need to buy all the clubs I see in a professional's bag?** Yes, if you are serious about the game. You might begin, however, with just a few, and then build up your set. For beginners I would recommend the driver, a three-wood, a four- or five-wood, a five-, seven- and nine-iron, plus the putter. (K. W.)

**If I play tennis, will that hurt my golf game?** No, it shouldn't, though some of the professional men find that tennis gives them too many bad habits. But for the country-club golfer tennis is fine. (B. B.)

**How can I tell distance?** By playing a course, plenty of practice and knowing the distance you can hit each club. We professionals walk off a course before playing, but that's not necessary for nontournament play. If you play your own course often, you'll soon learn the distances. (M. M.)

# Glossary of Terms

ADDRESS—Position assumed to hit the golf ball. Back is fairly straight and bent slightly from the hips. Feet are spaced the same as width of the shoulders. Body weight is distributed from the balls of the feet to the heels.

APRON—The two- or three-foot border around the green, slightly finer cut than fairway grass.

BIRDIE—One stroke less than par.

BOGEY—One stroke more than par.

BUNKER—Now means any sand trap. Traditionally the name of the fairway trap.

CHOKING THE CLUB—Placing the hands one or more inches down the shaft of the club, used to control the golf club better.

CLOSED STANCE—Left foot is forward at the address and closed to the line of flight.

DIVOT—The turf cut from the ground under the ball.

FADE—The ball curves slightly from left to right in the course of the flight.

FAIRWAY—The cut grass from tee to green where ball is to be played.

FIRM LEFT SIDE—The straight but not stiff left arm, wrist and leg. The golf swing begins with these key elements.

HAZARD—Any natural part of the course that must be overcome or avoided: sand traps, water, trees.

HITTING IT FAT—Hitting turf first and then the ball.

HOOK—The ball when driven curves to the left. A hooking ball has overspin on it.

LATERAL MOVEMENT—A slide or shift of the majority of body weight from one side of the body to the other, but without a pivot.

OPEN STANCE—Left foot is pulled back off the line two or three inches.

222

OVERLAPPING GRIP—Little finger of the right hand overlaps the forefinger of the left hand on the shaft.

PAR—The score that a good golfer would be expected to make on a given hole. Par according to yardage for women: up to 210, par 3; 211-400, par 4; 401-575, par 5; 576 and over, par 6.

PIVOT—The turning of the body that coils the power. It is a movement of the body weight from left to right, then back again.

PULL—Means the same as hook, but usually the ball drifts to the left instead of curving.

READING THE GREEN—Deciding which way the roll will break on the green.

ROUGH—High-cut grass bordering the fairway on both sides.

SLICE—Ball curves to the left, usually dramatically.

SQUARE STANCE—Feet, hips and shoulders are parallel with an imaginary line going straight back and straight through to the target.

SWINGING PLANE—The level of the swing, particularly the backswing.

TEE—The raised flat mound from which the drive is made.

TEMPO—The steady speed or rhythm of the swing as a whole.

TIGHT LIE—Little room behind the ball in which to place the club.

TOUCH—An ability to "feel" how hard a putt should be hit. Also, ability to play from around green.

TRAP SHOT—A shot from sand, with either a wood or an iron.

UNPLAYABLE LIE—A ball in such a position that it can't be played.